INDIA AND ITS INHABITANTS

INDIA AND ITS INHABITANTS

BY

CALEB WRIGHT, A. M.

THE AUTHOR VISITED INDIA AND TRAVELED EXTENSIVELY THERE, FOR THE EXPRESS PURPOSE OF COLLECTING THE INFORMATION CONTAINED IN THIS VOLUME.

THIRTY-FIRST THOUSAND

ILLUSTRATED BY NUMEROUS ENGRAVINGS

GYAN

Published by

Gyan Publishing House
5, Ansari Road
Daryaganj, New Delhi-110002
Phone: 011-47034999, 9811692060
E-mail: books@gyanbooks.com

Distribution Network
gyanbooks.com
India, USA, Canada, UK, Australia, France

ISBN : 978-81-212-3579-2 (PB)
First Published, 1857

2nd Impression 2020

Printed at: Gyan Press, Delhi.

India and its Inhabitants
Author: Caleb Wright

INDIA AND ITS INHABITANTS.

BY

CALEB WRIGHT, A. M.

THE AUTHOR VISITED INDIA AND TRAVELED EXTENSIVELY THERE, FOR THE EXPRESS PURPOSE OF COLLECTING THE INFORMATION CONTAINED IN THIS VOLUME.

THIRTY-FIRST THOUSAND.

ILLUSTRATED BY NUMEROUS ENGRAVINGS.

CINCINNATI, OHIO:
PUBLISHED BY J. A. BRAINERD.
1857.

TESTIMONIALS.

From Rev. Rufus Anderson, D.D., of Boston.

"Mr. Caleb Wright visited India a few years since, to qualify himself for lecturing on the manners and customs of the people in that country; and the Lectures he has since published give evidence of the carefulness of his observations, and of his faithfulness in description. The volume entitled LIFE IN INDIA is valuable for its subject-matter, even beyond any other similar collection of the size within my knowledge."

From Rev. Jeremiah Day, D.D., LL.D., formerly President of Yale College.

"Mr. Wright has recently lectured in seven of the churches in this city (New Haven), to large and highly gratified audiences. I believe his Lectures are doing much good, and hope they will continue to receive the patronage they deserve."

While Mr. Wright was lecturing in the principal cities and towns in the United States, testimonials, similar to the above, were received from a great number of persons in eminent stations, among whom were twenty Presidents of Colleges and Theological Seminaries, viz.:

Rev. E. Nott, D.D., ······ President of Union College.
L. Beecher, D.D., ··· President of Lane Seminary.
J. Edwards, D.D., ··· President (formerly) of Theol. Sem. Andover.
Jere. Day, LL.D., ··· President (formerly) of Yale College.
H. Humphrey, D.D., President (formerly) of Amherst College.
Mark Hopkins, D.D.,· President of Williams College.
S. North, LL.D., ··· President of Hamilton College.
Joel Parker, D.D.,·· President of Union Theol. Seminary, N. Y.
B. Tyler, D.D., · · · President of Theol. Seminary at E. Windsor
B. Sears, D.D., ····· President of Theol. Seminary at Newton.
R. Babcock, D.D., ··· President (formerly) of Waterville College.
J. Bates, D.D.,······ President (formerly) of Middlebury College.
N. Bangs, D.D.,····· President (formerly) of Wesleyan University.
H. J. Clark, A.M.,··· President of Alleghany College.
J. Carnahan, D.D.,··· President of Princeton College.
Asa Mahan, A.M.,··· President of Oberlin Institute.
E. W. Gilbert, D.D, · President of Delaware College.
Benjamin Hale, D.D., President of Geneva College.
Silas Totten, D.D.,··· President of Trinity College.
Hon. A. Hasbrouck, LL.D., President of Rutgers College.

ENGRAVINGS.

LECTURES ON INDIA.

LECTURE ON WOMEN.

Commencing at Page 129.

DESCRIPTION OF THE THUGS.

Commencing at Page 169.

DESCRIPTION OF FESTIVALS.

Commencing at Page 201.

SPECIMENS OF THE SHASTERS.

Commencing at Page 237.

ENGRAVING, No. 1. *Portrait of a Devotee who had been standing eight years, day and night.* *See description at page 73.*

No. 2. *Portrait of a Devotee who had kept the left arm elevated in the position represented until it had become stiff, and the finger-nails had grown six or eight inches in length.* *See page 70.*

No. 3. *Portrait of a Devotee who had kept both arms elevatsd until they had become stiff and immovable.* *See page 70.*

No. 4. *A Hindu of Bengal, of high rank, in full dress.*

No. 5 *A Mohammedan of Bengal, of high rank, in full dress.*

No. 6. *A Byragee.* *See page 69.*

No. 7. *Mohman Khaun, Nabob of Cambay.*

No. 8. *A Culi Chief. The Culis are a tribe of Robbers and Pirates in the north-west part of Hindustan.*

No. 9. *A Culi Soldier of the Forests of Rajputana.*

No. 10. THE GREAT MINARET AT DELHI.

This beautiful and magnificent tower is 242 feet in height. In the interior is a spiral staircase, leading to the different balconies, and to the top. It was built in the thirteenth century, but for what purpose is now unknown.

No. 11. SPECIMEN OF ARCHITECTURE AT BENARES.

Two of the eight columns which support the vestibule of a Temple, represented by engraving, No. 34, page 75.

No. 12. SPECIMEN OF HINDU ARCHITECTURE AT BAROLLI.

These Columns are in the immediate vicinity of a very large and beautiful temple, now in ruins. They probably supported a swing for the recreation of the god. See engraving, representing the swinging of Krishna, page 111.

No. 13. A TEMPLE AT MAHABALIPOORAM.

Each of the four columns is composed of a single stone. During certain Festivals an Image of Vishnu is brought from a larger temple and placed in this edifice to receive the homage of his votaries.

No. 14. *Temple of Elephanta.*

No. 15. *A Mosque at Delhi.*

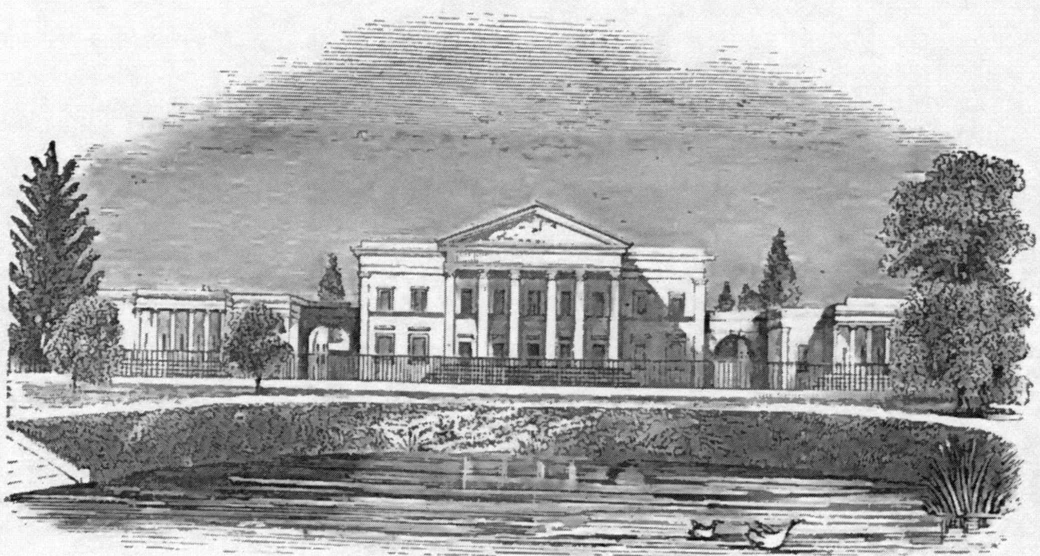

No. 16. *The Hindu College at Calcutta.*

No. 17. *Fort of Haje Ka, on the Indus*

No. 18. *Town and Fort of Roree, on the Indus.*

No. 19. *Fort of Burkhur, on the Indus.*

LECTURES ON INDIA.

LECTURE I.

It is the opinion of some eminent geographers, that India, under the name of *Tarshish*, was known in the days of Solomon, and celebrated as the land of spices, gold, and precious stones; but, whether it be the Tarshish of the ancients or not, it has for a long time been justly regarded with great interest. Here, vast and powerful empires have successively sprung up and flourished, while Europe was in a state of barbarism. Long before Christianity shed its light upon the world, India was the land of science and the arts. At the present time, however, its prominent characteristics are ignorance, poverty, and superstition.

It is not my purpose to direct your attention to the whole of India, but only to that portion of it usually denominated Hindustan, or India within the Ganges. This is a large peninsula, projecting into the Indian Ocean, south-west of the Chinese Empire, from which it is separated by the Himalaya Mountains. With a territory about as large as Mexico, it is supposed to contain a population of one hundred and thirty millions, or more inhabitants than England, Scotland, Ireland, Russia, and the continent of America.

The Hindus are of various dissimilar races, differing materially in stature, complexion, manners, language, and general character The Rajpoots and mountaineers of the north are large and of great muscular strength, while the inhabitants farther south are generally of small stature and of slender form. In complexion, they vary from a dark olive approaching to black, to a light, transparent, beautiful brown, resembling that of the natives of Northern Italy.

They are very fond of ornaments, such as rings in the ears and nose, with bracelets on the arms and ankles; yet their dress is exceedingly simple. See Engravings, Nos. 20 and 22.

The dress of the male consists of two pieces of cotton cloth, each containing about two yards. The one, called the *dhotee*, is girt about the loins and extends to the ankles. The other, called the *chadder*, is worn over the shoulders. The dress of the female is called a *saree*, and consists of a single piece of cloth of from four to seven yards. One end of this piece is wrapped around the loins, the width reaching to the feet; the other is gracefully thrown around the shoulders. In some parts of the country, it also covers the head. The children wear no clothing until they are from five to eight years of age; but they are frequently decorated with ornaments and jewels of considerable value.

The food of this people, with but few exceptions, is vegetable The use of animal food is denied them by their religion, unless the animals be first sacrificed to some idol. At their meals, they use neither tables, chairs, knives, forks, nor spoons. They sit upon the floor, and put the food into the mouth with the fingers of the right hand. They take their drink from a brass cup, which they never touch with the lips, but pour the liquid into the mouth. Fermented and distilled liquors are used only by the lowest castes; but the use of tobacco is almost universal, and here, as elsewhere has a most pernicious influence. Many of both sexes chew betel, a drug more filthy, if possible, than tobacco itself.

Most of the Hindu dwellings are rude huts, See Engraving, Number 20. The usual size is about eighteen feet long and twelve wide. The walls are built of mud, and the roof is thatched with straw or with the leaves of the palm. In cities, however, and in large villages, to prevent damage by fire, tiles are used instead of thatch. The cost of such dwellings varies from five to twenty dollars, according to the size and manner of finish. About one house in a thousand is built of durable materials, such as brick or stone. In cities they may be found from two to four stories high. These have flat roofs, and are built around a court or open space in the centre. In some houses, the court is very large, and is decorated with fountains, trees, and flowering shrubs. Most of the windows open into the court. As Hindu dwellings have few or no windows towards the street, they appear very much like prisons; and, in some respects, they are prisons; for within their walls the females are incarcerated for life. Such is the jealousy of their husbands, that they are never to be seen in the streets or in any

No. 20. *Hindu Family and Dwelling.*

No. 21. *Travelling in a Palankeen.*

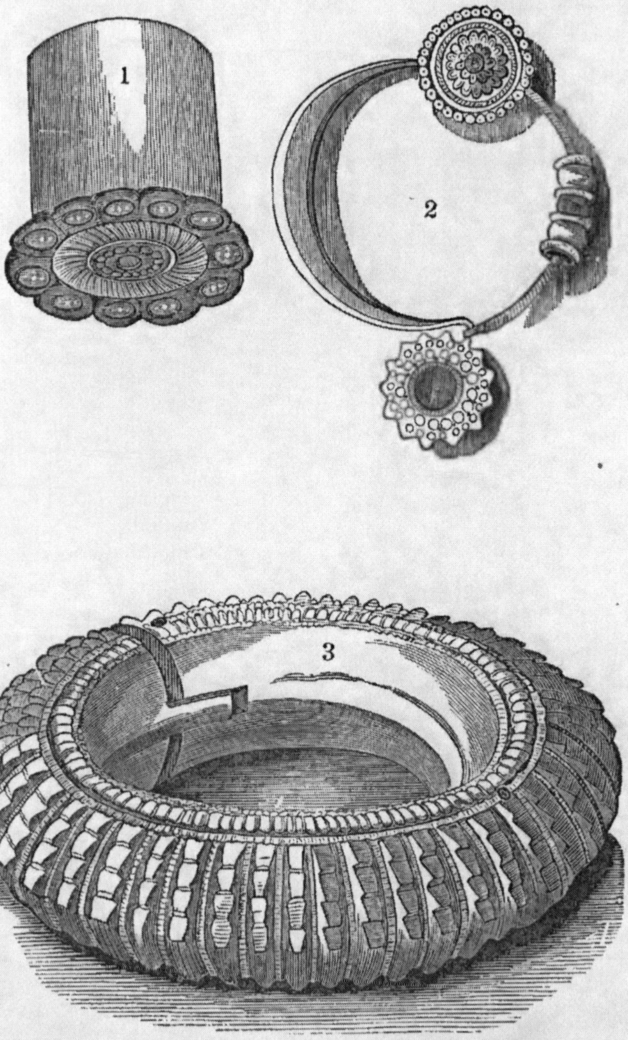

No. 22. JEWELRY—FROM SPECIMENS COLLECTED BY THE AUTHOR

These engravings are of the size of the objects which they represent. No. 1 is an ornament for the ear; the lobe of the ear is pierced, and the aperture gradually stretched until it becomes sufficiently large to admit the ornament. No. 2 is a nose jewel. No. 3 is a bracelet; it is made of brass, and weighs one pound and nine ounces. Some of the women deck the arms with from ten to twenty brass rings, weighing more than half a pound each.

public assembly. It is only the higher class of females, however, who are kept thus secluded; among the common people, women are to be seen at work in the fields, or going to market with large bundles of wood, or other heavy burdens, borne upon the head.

In engraving, No. 21 you have a representation of the usual method of travelling. With but few exceptions, there are no roads; consequently, wheel carriages are seldom used. This vehicle is called a *palankeen*. On the sides are sliding doors or venetians. Its construction in other respects will be readily understood. The usual number of bearers is eight. Four of these carry the palankeen thirty or forty rods; then the others take it upon their shoulders; thus, alternately, they relieve each other. Beside the bearers, several other men are employed to carry the baggage and to bear lighted torches by night. The bearers and other assistants are changed once in about ten miles, or as often as stage-drivers change their horses. The traveller proceeds on his journey from seventy to ninety miles in twenty-four hours, at an expense of about twenty-five cents per mile.

No. 24 is a Brahmin engaged in reading and explaining a poem containing some hundred thousand stanzas written on palm-leaf. It is one of many others equally voluminous, and has been handed down from generation to generation for more than three thousand years; it is written in Sanscrit, a dead language of a "wonderful construction — more perfect than the Greek, more copious than the Latin, and more exquisitely refined than either." It is a portion of the Holy Vedas. In a peculiar tone of voice, he chants the sacred text, stopping at the end of each stanza to translate and explain. His hearers listen attentively to the exciting narrative, now convulsed with laughter at some dexterous exploit, and then thrilled with horror at some dreadful calamity. All the religious books of the Hindus, including the four Vedas, are called *Shasters*.* They are so numerous that an entire human life would not be sufficient for an attentive perusal of them.

No. 23 is a celebration of the Huli festival. On this occasion, the people of all classes use the most obscene and abusive language, and, by means of large syringes, bespatter each other with

* See "Specimens of the Shasters or Sacred Books of the Brahmins, consisting of Songs Legendary Tales, &c.," page 247 of this volume.

colored water; they also pelt each other with red and yellow powder, and with the mud and filth of the streets. Should a Hindu be asked why he conducts in this manner at the time of the Huli, he would say, "It is our custom, and it can be proved from the Shasters that it has been the custom of our forefathers for millions of generations." To the mind of a Hindu, whatever is customary is proper; for he believes that the customs of his forefathers, civil, social, and religious, were instituted by the gods, and are therefore incapable of improvement. The effect of this belief is to keep every thing stationary. There is no progress in knowledge—no change for the better in any department in life. The fashion of dress, the form of agricultural and mechanical instruments, the manner of erecting habitations, and the performance of various kinds of labor, are the same as they were thousands of years ago. This fact may be illustrated by an anecdote. An English gentleman devised various plans of introducing improvements; among others, he wished to substitute wheelbarrows for the baskets in which the natives carry burdens on their heads. He caused several of these useful articles to be constructed, and labored with much assiduity to introduce them among his workmen. In his presence, they used them with apparent cheerfulness, and even admitted that they were far preferable to the baskets. The gentleman was delighted with his success. On one occasion, however, having been absent a few hours, on returning somewhat unexpectedly, he was surprised to find all his laborers carrying the wheelbarrows filled with earth on their heads.

Their unyielding attachment to ancient customs is the natural result of their religious belief. Any change, however slight, in the mode of labor or business, is a violation of religious duty. It is evident, therefore, that the comforts and improvements of civilized life can never be introduced among the Hindus until they become convinced of the falsity of their Shasters and the foolishness of their traditions. The first step in the process of reform and improvement is to renounce that system of religion which for thousands of years has held them in the most cruel bondage.

The subject of engraving, No. 26 is beautifully sculptured on the surface of a large rock in the Ganges, and is also frequently represented by the Hindus in their paintings. An enormous serpent, having many heads, is coiled up in such a manner as to form a couch, upon which a Hindu divinity is sleeping. It illustrates a familiar legend in their Shasters. After the destruction of a

No. 23. *Celebrating the Huli Festival.*

No. 24. A Brahmin reading the Shasters.

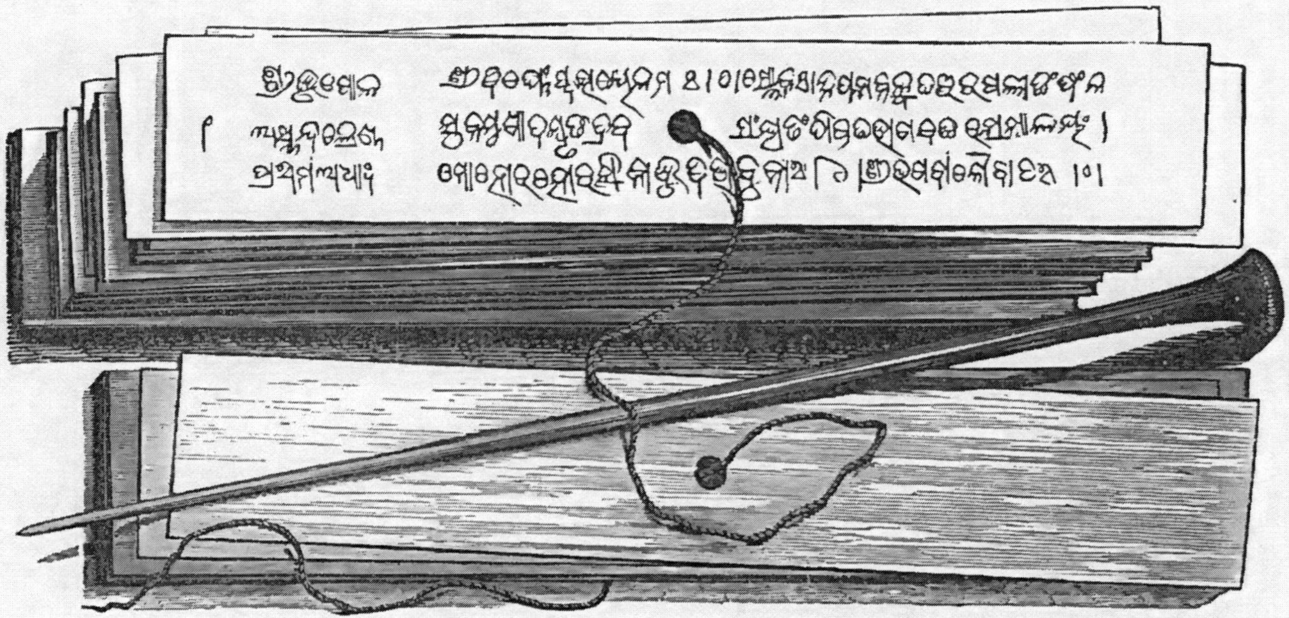

No. 25. A BOOK AND AN IRON STYLE USED IN WRITING

In the middle and southern parts of Hindustan, books are written on palm leaf. A volume of ordinary size is about eighteen inches in length, two in width, and four in thickness. The one represented by the engraving is only six inches in length. It is in the Orea language, and is open at the first page, exhibiting a fac-simile of the writing.

former world by a deluge, this divinity, whose name is Vishnu, composed himself to sleep on a thousand-headed serpent, which floated upon the surface of the waters; during a nap of some millions of years, a water-lily grew from his body; from this flower issued Brahma, the Creator. Having formed the world anew and created many of the gods, he proceeded to create man, when the four classes or castes into which the Hindus are divided issued from different parts of his body: the Brahmins from his head, the Kshutryus from his arms, the Voishnus from his breast, while the Shudras had their ignoble origin in his feet; agreeably to which legend, the Brahmins are supposed to be entitled to a very high rank, while the Shudras are hardly regarded as human beings. These four classes have, from various causes, been divided into more than two hundred distinct castes. If one of high caste violate the rules of his community, he cannot receive an honorable dismission, and enter a lower caste, but is forever excluded from all respectable society; repentance and reformation have no tendency to restore him. One of low caste, though ever so learned, wise, or virtuous, can make no approximation to a higher caste. The distance between the Shudra, the lowest caste, and the Brahmin, is immeasurably great; the Brahmin cannot even instruct the Shudra, but with the greatest precaution, lest he should be defiled. But, low as the Shudra is, he has an honorable standing in society when compared with the Parriahs, a race who are not regarded as having any caste. They, when walking in the street, must keep on the side opposite the sun, lest their filthy shadows should fall upon the consecrated Brahmin. It is not uncommon to see the lower castes prostrating themselves as worshippers at the feet of the Brahmin, and greedily drinking the water which he has condescended to sanctify by the immersion of his great toe.

The pernicious influence of caste is strikingly illustrated by an incident related to me by Rev. Mr. Day, a missionary at Madras. As he was riding through a native village, he saw a woman .ying by the side of the street, apparently in the agonies of death; she had lain there about twenty-four hours, and, during all this time, the villagers had been constantly passing and repassing, without manifesting the least interest or sympathy. When Mr. Day asked them why they thus neglected this woman, and suffered her to lie there and die, they replied, "Why should we take care of her? She does not belong to our caste." A little rice-water, it appears, had been offered her, but she would not drink it, simply because the person offering it belonged to a lower caste. Had she tasted the rice-water, or eaten any food cooked by these villagers, or even drank pure water from their vessels, she would have lost caste. And what then? Her own children would have fled from her as from one infected with the plague; her husband would not have permitted her to enter his house; even the parental roof would not have afforded her an asylum for a single moment; had any friends or relatives dared to associate with her, they too would have lost caste and been involved in the same disgrace. Thus she would necessarily become an outcast and a vagabond.

In most of the large houses in India, there is an apartment which serves as a family chapel. Engraving, No. 27 represents such an apartment in a very elegantly-finished house in the city of Benares. In the farther part of the chapel is the altar or shrine on which the idols are placed. Each member of the family is expected to offer up his devotions to these idols every morning and evening.

According to their own standard, the Hindus are preëminently a religious people. The number of their gods, as stated in their Shasters, is three hundred and thirty millions. These fabled gods are not represented as acting in concert; they fight and quarrel with each other, and with their wives and children, murder the innocent for the sake of plunder, and commit crimes, the bare recital of which to a Christian audience would excite the utmost horror and disgust.

It is generally admitted, that neither nations nor individuals aim at greater purity of morals than their religion requires. We may expect to find any community below, rather than above this standard. This is true in regard to the Hindus. Their gods and goddesses being extremely vicious, the manner in which they are worshipped must correspond with their character; it cannot be expected that the moral character of the people should be other than it is, a compound of every thing that is debasing. Gross and polluted as their divinities are, they are yet too refined and elevated, in their estimation, to be worshipped without imagery. Images are made in forms as various, unnatural, and horrid, as the imagination can conceive. When one of them is consecrated by the Brahmin, the divinity for whom it is designed is supposed to take up his abode in it, and is propitious or unpropitious according to the manner in which it is worshipped.

The goddess Kali, (See Number 29) is represented as a woman of a dark blue color, with four arms, in the act of trampling under her feet her prostrate and supplicating husband. In one hand

No. 26. *Vishnu, reposing on his Serpent Couch.*

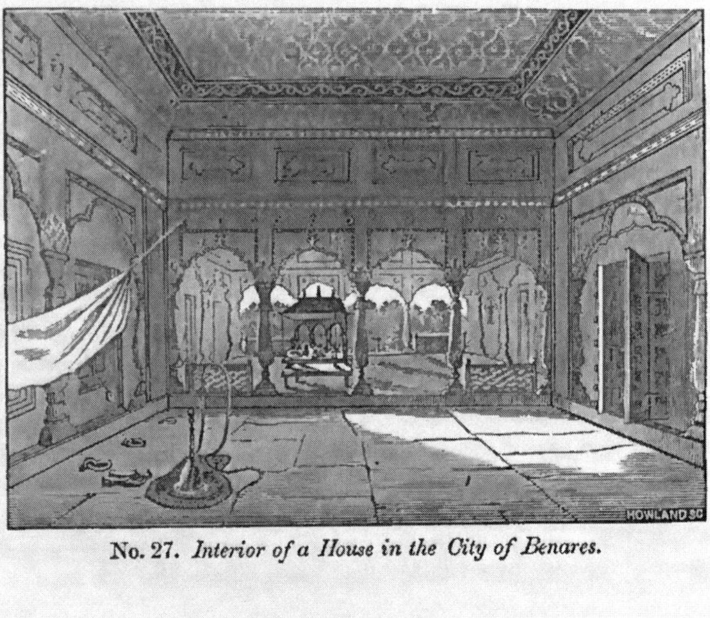

No. 27. *Interior of a House in the City of Benares.*

she holds the bloody head of a giant, and in another an exterminating sword. Her long, dishevelled hair reaches to her feet; her tongue protrudes from her distorted mouth; and her lips, eyebrows, and breast, are stained with the blood of the victims of her fury, whom she is supposed to devour by thousands. Her ear ornaments are composed of human carcasses. The girdle about her waist consists of the bloody hands of giants slain by her in single combat, and her necklace is composed of their skulls. This monster divinity is one of the most popular objects of Hindu worship. She calls forth the shouts, the acclamations, and the free-will offerings of myriads of infatuated worshippers. Her temples are continually drenched with the blood of victims; even human victims are occasionally sacrificed to her. In 1828, the Rajah of the Goands sacrificed twenty men at one time, as the promised reward of her supposed assistance in a single enterprise.

The Hindus, like the inhabitants of more civilized countries, have secret societies. The most remarkable of these is the society of the Thugs, which boasts of great antiquity. In some respects, it is a religious society; for its members believe that they are under the immediate guidance and protection of Kali, and that she permits them to obtain their livelihood by murdering travellers on the highway and then taking their property. It would be quite inconsistent with their religious principles, to rob any person until he is first deprived of life by strangulation. They affirm that this system was instituted by Kali, and is consequently of divine origin; that, for many thousands of years, she assisted them in escaping detection, by devouring the dead bodies of their victims; but, on a certain occasion, a Thug, contrary to her command, looked back to see how she disposed of the corpses, and saw her feasting on them. This circumstance so offended her, that she declared she would no longer devour those whom they murdered. They believe, however, that she still continues to assist them, and that she directs their movements by certain omens. When, therefore, they are about to commence their excursions, in order to propitiate the favor of Kali, they sacrifice a sheep, by cutting off its head, upon which the priest pours water and repeats the following prayer: "Great Goddess! Universal Mother! If this our meditated expedition is fitting in thy sight, vouchsafe us thine help and the signs of thy approbation." While repeating this invocation, they watch the head of the victim; if they observe tremulous or convulsive motions in the mouth and nostrils, it is to them the sign that Kali approves their expedition. When about to murder a traveller, if they hear or see any thing which, according to their superstitious notions, indicates evil, they allow him to pass on unmolested; but if the omen is esteemed good, they regard it as a positive command to murder him. In 1826, the East India Company adopted measures to suppress this system of wholesale murder. Since that time, between two and three thousand Thugs have been arrested, tried, and convicted. Two hundred and six were convicted at a single session of the court. It appeared, in the course of the evidence, that these prisoners, at different times, had murdered four hundred and forty persons. In view of these facts, who is prepared to carry out the doctrine, that it matters not what a man believes, if he is only sincere?

Engraving, No. 28 is a view of one of the most celebrated temples in India. It is devoted to the worship of Kali, and is situated at Kali Ghat, three miles from Calcutta. The small building on the left, and the other on the right, are temples of Shiva.

In Calcutta, the missionaries have established several schools, which are in a flourishing condition. The one under the superintendence of Rev. Dr. Duff is attended by more than a thousand young men, belonging to the most respectable families in the city. Kali Prasanna Mukarje, one of the young men educated at the mission schools, is a "Kulin Brahmin of the highest caste, and, on his mother's side, is a Holdar Brahmin. The Holdars are the original proprietors of Kali Ghat, and the hereditary officiating priests of the temple, to whom all the offerings at this shrine of idolatry belong. Kali Prasanna is heir to his mother's property, being her only son; he is also heir to his uncle, who is a Zemindar, and one of the proprietors of the temple of Kali; and, by marriage, he is heir to his father-in-law's property. He is thus the only male representative of three ancient and highly-respectable families, and, by inheritance, would have been the principal proprietor of Kali Ghat and the high priest of the temple." Besides what he was to inherit, he possessed property to the amount of about one hundred thousand dollars. He was fully aware that, should he become a Christian, he would, by the laws of his country, not only be deprived of his property, but would be despised by his countrymen, forsaken by his relatives, and regarded as an outcast. Yet he gave up all, was baptized, and became a member of one of the mission churches. At various missionary stations which I visited were several other Brahmins, who had forfeited their title to large estates by becoming Christians.

No. 28. *A Temple of Kali, near Calcutta.*

No. 29. *The Goddess Kali.*

The figure on the left of engraving, No. 31, was found among some ruins in Behar. It is an image of Shiva, who, according to Hindu mythology, is the husband of Kali. He has eight arms and three eyes, one of which is in the centre of his forehead. The serpent with which he is decorated is rearing its head over his right shoulder. With one foot he is crushing an enemy in the act of drawing a sword; with two of his hands he is tossing a human victim on the points of a trident; in a third he holds a drum, in a fourth an axe, in a fifth a sword, in a sixth a portion of the Vedas, and in a seventh a club, on the end of which is a human head.

The figure on the right was copied from a sculpture on the wall of a temple at Gaya. It has four legs, sixteen arms, and seven heads. Its girdle and crown are ornamented with heads. In each hand it has an animal on a plate, as if dressed for food. It is dancing on four men's bodies, two prostrated and two ready to be crushed. Above, beneath, and on each side, were armed female furies dancing on human carcasses; but these are not copied into the engraving. By the inhabitants of Gaya, this image is called *Mahamaya*, another name for Kali; but it is a male, and, perhaps, was originally intended to represent her husband, Shiva.

In the month of April, a festival in honor of Shiva is celebrated in almost every town and village. One of these festivals I witnessed in Calcutta. On the first day, at sunset, the worshippers assembled at different places, and danced, to the sound of drums and other rude and noisy music, before an image of Shiva. Then, one after another, they were suspended from a beam, with the head downward, over a fire. The next day, about five o'clock in the afternoon, each company reassembled and erected a stage about ten feet in height, from which they threw themselves upon large knives. The knives being placed in a sloping position, the greater part of the thousands that fall upon them escape unhurt; but occasionally an individual is cruelly mangled. About forty persons threw themselves from one stage. None but the last appeared to receive much injury. He pretended to be killed, and was carried off with great shouting. During the whole of the night, Calcutta resounded with the sound of gongs, drums, trumpets, and the boisterous shouts of the worshippers. Early the next morning, forty or fifty thousand persons were assembled on the adjoining plain. Processions, accompanied by music, were passing and repassing in every direction. In the processions many persons were daubed over with the sacred ashes of cows' ordure. Hundreds of these were inflicting self-torture. In one procession, I saw ten persons, each with more than a hundred iron pins inserted in the flesh. In another, each devotee had a cluster of artificial serpents fastened with iron pins to his naked back. In other processions, many had the left arm perforated, for the insertion of rods from five to fifteen feet in length. These rods were kept in constant and quick motion through the flesh, to increase the pain. Some had their tongues pierced, for the insertion of similar rods, which were occasionally drawn rapidly up and down through the tongue. One man, having a rod fifteen feet long, and, at the largest end, nearly one inch in diameter, commencing with the smaller end, drew the whole rod through his tongue. After wiping the blood from it upon his garment, he thrust it again into his tongue. Others were drawing living serpents through their tongues and dancing around like maniacs. In the streets through which the processions passed were devotees, with their sides pierced; a rope passed through each incision, and the ends of the two ropes were fastened to four stakes driven into the earth. In this condition, the infatuated creatures dance backward and forward, drawing the ropes, at each movement, through their lacerated flesh. On the afternoon of the next day, swinging machines were erected at the places of concourse. They consisted of a perpendicular post, about twenty-five feet high, upon the top of which was a transverse beam, balanced on its centre, and turning on a pivot. A rope was attached to one end of this beam, by which the other could be elevated or depressed at pleasure. From this end, many of the worshippers were suspended by iron hooks inserted into the muscular parts of their backs. I have in my possession a pair of hooks which have been used for that purpose. These hooks I saw thrust into a man's naked back. The rope attached to them was made fast to the beam of the machine, by which he was lifted up twenty-five or thirty feet from the earth. It was then put in a circular motion on its pivot, and the poor sufferer made to swing with great rapidity for some minutes. Thousands and tens of thousands, annually, are thus cruelly tortured on these machines.

No. 30. *A Temple at Tanjore.*

No. 32 is a temple of Shiva, which I saw near Allahabad. It is surrounded by a high mound, composed wholly of the fragments of earthen bottles. On one of the last days of February, from twenty to forty thousand pilgrims assemble, each being provided with two or three earthen bottles, containing water from the Ganges, and a few copper coins. Such is the offering they make to Shiva; and, believing him to be greatly pleased with the act, they dash and break the bottles against the temple. The next day, the Brahmins, faithful and true to Shiva, do not forget to pick up the money, and, as the trustees of the idol, keep it for him. That the temple may not be buried beneath the fragments of this novel offering, and that no coin may escape their vigilance, they also have the broken bottles removed to a short distance, where they had accumulated to the extent here represented. It cannot be difficult to understand why this peculiar mode of worship was invented by the Brahmins. It may also serve as an illustration of the manner in which they take advantage of the credulity of the people and secure a large amount of property.

The two figures in engraving 33 are portraits of individuals whom I had the opportunity of frequently seeing. The one on the left is the portrait of a religious mendicant. The number of mendicants in India amounts to many hundreds of thousands. As a religious duty, they forsake their families and friends, renounce every useful occupation, and wander from place to place, begging their food. They are literally clothed with filth and rags; the latter, in many instances, being less in quantity than the former. Some of them are decorated with large quantities of false hair, strings of human bones, and artificial snakes. Others carry a human skull containing a most filthy mixture. If no money or food be given them by those persons of whom they solicit alms, they profess to eat the filth out of the skull, as an act of revenge. One sect of them, professing to be extremely anxious to avoid destroying animal life, carry a broom, composed of soft cotton threads, gently to sweep the insects from their path. They also erect hospitals for the reception of aged, sick, and lame animals. There is an institution of this kind in the vicinity of Bombay, which, in 1840, contained from fifty to one hundred horses, one hundred and seventy-five oxen and cows, and two hundred dogs, beside cats, monkeys, and reptiles. It has been said that paganism never erected a hospital; but this is not quite true. I believe, however, that these are the only hospitals that have been erected by the worshippers of idols.

There is another sect of mendicants, who are worshippers of Krishna. Though men, they put on the dress and ornaments, and assume the manners, of milkmaids. This is supposed to be very pleasing to the object of their worship; for, when he was on earth, he is said to have been very partial to the milkmaids, and to have married no fewer than sixteen thousand of them.

The other figure on the same engraving is a portrait of Puri-Suttema, an individual with whom I was well acquainted. For seven years he had been a religious mendicant. At length he read a Christian tract entitled "A Precept to the Inhabitants of this Part of the World, by the Missionaries." "By studying it," said he, "I found there was a great difference between the notions I had imbibed and the virtuous precepts contained in that book; I plainly saw that my former way was all deception, and that this book pointed out a better." He embraced that better way, and is now a preacher of the gospel.

Many religious mendicants subject themselves to various modes of self-torture. Engravings, Nos. 1, 2 and 3 are portraits of individuals, selected as specimens of this class of persons.

The devotee represented by engraving, No. 2 I saw at a festival on the banks of the Ganges. He had kept his left arm thus elevated until it had become stiff and permanently fixed, the muscles and sinews had lost all power of producing motion, and the flesh had become withered. The finger-nails, as you perceive, had grown to the enormous length of six or eight inches. During my residence in Hindustan, I saw as many as nine persons with their arms elevated in the position here delineated.

The devotee represented by engraving, No. 3 has both arms elevated. This man I saw frequently in the city of Benares. In answer to my inquiries relative to his history, I was told that, in the earlier part of his life, he served as a soldier; but, having lost his right leg, he became unfit for the duties of the army. In order to secure a livelihood, as well as a large stock of religious merit, he turned devotee. Having substituted a wooden leg in the place of the one lost, he took a small idol in each hand, and elevated them above his head until his arms became perfectly stiff and immovable.

No. 31. *Shiva.* *Mahamaya.*

No. 32. *A Temple of Shiva.*

It may, perhaps, seem impossible, that a man should be able, by his own voluntary act, to keep his arms in this unnatural position. One would suppose that in sleep, at least, the limbs would resume their proper posture. In the first part of the process, it becomes necessary to fasten the arms to poles lashed to the body; but it requires no great length of time so to paralyze the muscles and sinews that they are no longer under the control of the mind.

The devotee represented by engraving No. 1 I also frequently saw at Benares. Under a wretched shed on the bank of the Ganges, he had been standing, day and night, for eight years. He had nothing to lean against but a piece of bamboo suspended by cords from the roof of his shed. His dress was a ragged woollen blanket saturated with filth. His face was smeared with the sacred ashes, his body greatly emaciated, while his feet and legs were so dropsical and swollen as to require bandages to prevent their bursting. Sometimes he slept as he stood, but generally he was awake and busily employed in his devotions. In his right hand he held a string of wooden beads contained in a red bag. Hour after hour he repeated the names of the gods, and at each repetition passed a bead between his thumb and finger. Occasionally he laid aside his beads, and with his finger wrote, on a board covered with ashes, the names of the idol gods upon whom he depended for happiness in a future life, as the reward of his self-inflicted miseries. In this manner he had spent the last eight years of his life. I asked him how long he intended to stand there. His reply was, "Until Gunga calls for me,"—meaning until death, when his body would be thrown into the River Gunga or Ganges.

On one occasion, I saw a devotee performing a pilgrimage to the Ganges in a manner somewhat peculiar. He prostrated himself at full length upon the ground, and, stretching forward his hands, laid down a small stone; he then struck his head three times against the earth, arose, walked to the stone, and, picking it up, again prostrated himself, as before; and thus continued to measure the road with his body. I was told by a missionary at Benares, that he had recently seen a devotee prostrating himself every six feet of the way towards the temple of Juggernaut, from which he was then four hundred miles distant, and that he was accompanied on his pilgrimage by a poor cripple, who, unable to walk, was crawling along on his hands and knees. Another devotee has been rolling upon the earth for the last nine years. He has undertaken to roll from Benares to Cape Comorin, a distance of one thousand five hundred miles, and more than half of the journey he has accomplished.

It is universally believed by the Hindus, that, if a man perform a pilgrimage, or swing upon hooks, or torture himself in any other manner, he will be rewarded for it, either in this life or in a future state of existence. No matter what the motive of the devotee may be; if he perform the service, he must receive the reward. As an illustration of this delusive theory, permit me to relate an anecdote from their sacred books.

Narayan is the name of a Hindu god. A certain man, notoriously wicked, having a son of that name, was laid upon a sick-bed. In the hour of death, being parched with a fever, he called upon his son to give him water. The son being disobedient, the father called again in anger, and expired. The messengers of Yumu, the god of the infernal regions, immediately seized him, and would have dragged him to the place of torment, but they were prevented by the servants of Narayan, who took him by force and carried him to heaven. The messengers of Yumu, in great rage, hastened to their master and told him what had transpired. Yumu ordered his recorder to examine his books. He did so, and found that the man in question was a great sinner. Yumu then repaired in person to Narayan and demanded an explanation. Narayan made this reply: "However sinful the man has been, in his last moments, and with his last breath, he repeated my name; and you, Yumu, ought to know that, if any man, either by design or accident, either in anger or derision, repeats my name with his last breath, he must go to heaven." The doctrine of this fable is literally and universally believed by the people. Hence, when a person is in the agonies of death, his friends exhort him to repeat the names of the gods; and, if he is so fortunate as to die with one of these names upon his lips, they consider it a sure passport to heaven. Many spend a large portion of their time in repeating the names of gods. Parrots are taught to do the same; and such a spokesman commands a great price, especially among business men, who imagine that, by owning such a parrot, their spiritual treasures are accumulating while they attend to their usual occupations.

The opposite engraving, No. 34, is a view in Benares, the holy city of the Hindus. It is situated upon the River Ganges, about eight hundred miles from its mouth, and, with a population of two hundred thousand, is estimated to contain one thousand temples. Benares is not only celebrated for the number of its temples, and the benefits they are supposed to confer, but for the learning and sanctity of its Brahmins, for its schools of science and the arts

No. 33. *Two Portraits.*

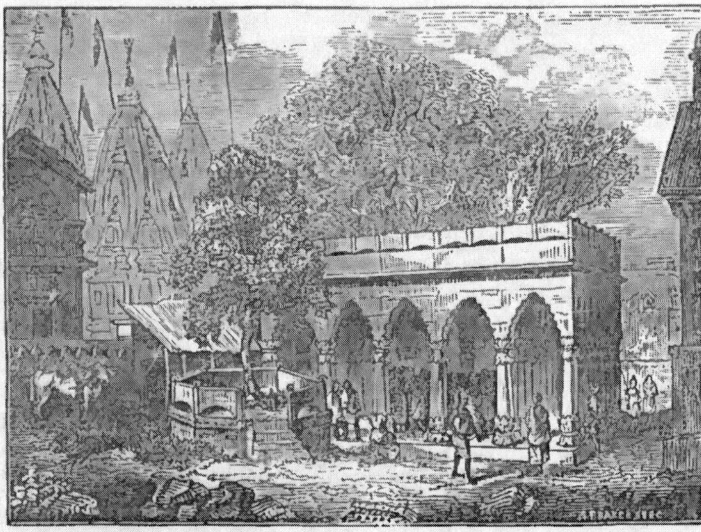

No. 34. *A View in the City of Benares.*

and, more especially, for its great antiquity. It is fabled to have been built by Shiva, of pure gold, but has long since degenerated into stone, brick, and clay, in consequence of the sins of the people. It is visited by more pilgrims than any other place in India. When travelling from Benares to Allahabad, a distance of only eighty miles, I estimated the number I saw by the way at twelve thousand, or one hundred and fifty to every mile.

The large building on the right, a part of which is to be seen, is a Mohammedan mosque. It stands upon the place once occupied by a very large and splendid Hindu temple, which contained an image of Shiva, said to have fallen on this spot from heaven. Soon after the commencement of the eighteenth century, Aurungzebe, a celebrated Mohammedan conqueror, demolished the temple and built this mosque. The Hindus say that the indignant idol, to escape the impious hands of the Mohammedans, while tearing down the temple, threw itself into a neighboring well. This circumstance rendered the water very holy and purifying. The well is in a spacious and beautiful pavilion, as represented near the centre of the engraving. It is built of stone, and consists of a roof supported by four rows of columns. On the left of the pavilion are three temples of a pyramidical form. The one in the centre is esteemed the most holy temple in Benares, because it contains the celebrated idol which concealed itself in the well. The Brahmins who officiate at this temple are also esteemed very holy. I will relate a few incidents illustrative of their character. They discovered that an aged pilgrim, who came there to worship, had a large sum of money about him. They told him that, if he would give them his money, and then, in the presence of the idol, cut his throat, the idol would immediately restore him to the vigor and freshness of youth. The deluded man believed them. He gave up all his money, entered the temple, called on the name of Shiva, and then cut his throat from ear to ear. Rev. Mr. Smith, who described to me this horrid transaction, saw him weltering in his blood. Mr. Smith also stated that, soon after he commenced his missionary labors in Benares, the Brahmins murdered a celebrated dancing girl in this temple, for the sake of the jewels which decorated her person. To prevent discovery, they cut off her head and threw it into the Ganges. They then cut her body into small pieces and strewed them about the streets, to be eaten by the dogs and vultures.

There are more than eight thousand religious mendicants in this city who live on charity. Those who belong to the sect called

Purumhunse have professedly attained to a state of perfection, and are worshipped as gods. They are readily distinguished by their long hair and beards, which are never trimmed or cleansed, and also by their dress, which is neither more comely nor substantial than that which was in fashion before garments were made by sewing together fig-leaves. These reputed gods sometimes come in contact with men who have not attained to their state of perfection. Some years since, Mr. Bird, an English magistrate of Benares, seeing a Purumhunse in his yard, ordered him to be gone, and threatened to horsewhip him if he ever saw him there again. A few days afterwards he came again, and found that Mr. Bird was faithful to his promise. The natives, who came running from every direction, were greatly enraged that an unholy foreigner should chastise one of their gods. Whatever power the whip may have had in exciting the wrath of this human god, still he did not dare to manifest it; for, had he uttered a single angry word, he would have lost all claim to perfection and divinity. He therefore said, with much apparent coolness and unconcern, "It is all right, it is perfectly right; for I recollect that, in a former birth, this magistrate was my donkey. I used to ride him beyond his strength, whip and abuse him, and now I am justly suffering for the sins thus committed."

Engraving, No. 36 illustrates a custom which prevails in the northern part of Bengal. I allude to a species of infanticide. When an infant declines in health, the mother imagines that it is under the influence of an evil spirit, to appease whose wrath, she places her child in a basket and suspends it from the branch of a tree in which evil spirits are supposed to reside. The infant is generally visited and fed by its mother for three days. If it be not devoured by ants nor birds of prey, nor die through exposure to the cold and the rain, it is afterwards taken home. In the vicinity of Malda, an infant thus exposed fell from its basket and was immediately seized by a prowling jackal. Fortunately, the Rev. Mr. Thomas happened to pass that way just in time to prevent the child from being devoured. He had the satisfaction of presenting it alive to its mother. On another occasion, as he was passing under the same tree, he found a basket suspended from its branches containing the skeleton of an infant, the flesh having been devoured by the white ants.

Among the Jerejas, a fierce and warlike tribe, who live in the north-west part of Hindustan, great numbers of female infants are

Presenting Offerings to a Mendicant Priest.

put to death immediately after birth. In one village, in which were twenty-two boys, not one girl was to be found. The villagers confessed that they had all been murdered. In another village were found fifty-eight boys and only four girls ; in another, forty-four boys and four girls ; and, in many other villages, the number of boys exceeded that of the girls in nearly the same proportion.

The Jerejas have a tradition, that a curse was once pronounced by a holy Brahmin upon all of their tribe who should suffer their female children to live. To escape the effects of this curse, and to avoid the trouble and expense of bringing up their daughters, whom they regard as worthless, they are induced to imbrue them hands in their innocent blood. Mothers are the executioners of their own children. They either strangle them or poison them with opium. That they should be the agents in sustaining so horrid a custom is the more extraordinary when the fact is known that they were born and brought up among other tribes, where female infants are reared with comparative kindness. But such is the debasing influence of heathenism, that natural affection is extinguished, and all the kind sympathies of the maternal heart give place to the most savage ferocity. The infant, after it is destroyed, is placed naked in a small basket, and carried out and interred by one of the female attendants.

The subject of engraving, number 37 is the interior of the mission chapel in the city of Cuttack, in the province of Orissa. It is an interesting fact, that this chapel stands upon the very spot where once stood a temple devoted to Shiva.

About one hundred miles south-west of Cuttack is the country of the Kunds. They worship a goddess called *Bhuenee.* To secure her blessing upon the soil they cultivate, they deem it important at certain times to offer human sacrifices upon her altars. The victims, who must be in the freshness and bloom of youth, are procured by stealing children from distant villages and rearing them until they become large enough to be acceptable to the goddess. At the time of sacrifice, the victim is tied to a post; the sacrificer, with an axe in his hand, slowly advances towards him, chanting to the goddess and her train the following hymn, which has been translated for me by Rev. Charles Lacy, one of the missionaries at Cuttack: —

"Hail, mother, hail! Hail, goddess Bhuenee!
Lo! we present a sacrifice to thee.
Partake thereof, and let it pleasure give,
And, in return, let us thy grace receive.
With various music on this festive day,
Lo! thee we honor, and thy rites obey.
Hail, all ye gods who in the mountain dwell,
In the wild jungle, or the lonely dell!
Come all together, come with one accord,
And eat the sacrifice we have prepared.
In all the fields and all the plots we sow,
O let a rich and plenteous harvest grow!
Ho, all ye gods and goddesses! give ear,
And be propitious to our earnest prayer.
Behold a youth for sacrifice decreed,
Blooming with tender flesh and flushed with blood!
No sire, no matron, rears him as a son;
His flesh, and blood, his life, and all, are thine.
Without the pale of sacred wedlock born,
We caught and reared him for thy rite alone.
Now, too, with rites from all pollution free,
We offer him, O Bhuenee! to thee."

As soon as this hymn is finished, with one blow of the axe the chest of the devoted youth is laid open. The sacrificer instantly thrusts in his hand and tears out the heart. Then, while the victim is writhing in the agonies of death, the multitude rush upon him, each one tearing out a part of his vitals or cutting off a piece of flesh from the bones; for, according to their superstitions, the pieces have no virtue unless they are secured before life is extinct. Immediately they hasten with their bloody treasure and bury it in their fields, expecting in this way to render them fruitful.

Please notice those boys sitting on the floor, according to native custom. There are ten of them, and they are Kunds. They had once been stolen from their parents, and were kept for the purpose of being sacrificed; and, had they not been rescued by the agents of the East India Company, they would have been destroyed in the manner just described. But now they attend the mission school during the week, and on the Sabbath they meet in this chapel to worship that God whose kind providence saved them from an early and cruel death.

Turn now to the young woman seated at the extreme left of the audience. She, also, when a child, was stolen from her

No. 36. *An Infant Victim of Superstition.*

No. 37. *Interior of a Chapel at Cuttack.*

parents and reserved for the slaughter. She was kept until she had attained her sixteenth year, and was rescued only four days before she was to have been offered in sacrifice. I heard the account of her sufferings from her own lips, and saw the scars made by the fetters with which she had been confined. But now she is a member of the mission church, and is exerting a happy influence in teaching others the way of life.

In the course of a few months, the agents of the East India Company rescued one hundred and eight children, whom the Kunds were preparing for sacrifice. It may with propriety be said, they were fattening them like beasts for the slaughter; for they believe that the goddess will not be pleased with the sacrifice of young men and women, unless they are healthy and blooming. How different this from the blessed training of our children in the Sabbath school, that they may present their bodies a living sacrifice to God! What a contrast between Paganism and Christianity! Here a Christian chapel has literally been built upon the ruins of a heathen temple. It has also been rebuilt and enlarged, to accommodate the increasing number of worshippers, more than one hundred of whom are communicants. What has produced this change? Why are not the cruel rites of Shiva still performed upon this spot? The humble and unobtrusive missionary has proclaimed the simple doctrines of the cross, and the Divine Spirit has blessed his labors.

Baber, the Founder of the Great Mogul Empire.

LECTURES ON INDIA

LECTURE II.

The attention of the traveller, in the south-western part of Asia, is frequently arrested by splendid edifices, and occasionally by large cities, long since deserted by their inhabitants. They were built by the Mohammedans, who, about the year one thousand, invaded India, and, by a long series of the most ferocious and cruel wars, established the great Mogul empire. This vast empire, and other extensive countries in Asia, have, within the last hundred years, been annexed to the British dominions.

Delhi, the residence of the Mogul emperors, is supposed to have been founded about three hundred years before the Christian era. In the course of a few centuries, it became the largest and most magnificent city in India. In 1398, Tamerlane, having slaughtered great numbers of the unoffending Hindus in battle, and murdered one hundred thousand who had surrendered as prisoners of war, besieged Delhi. The city surrendered, was pillaged and almost destroyed. Delhi, however, not only recovered from this calamity, but attained to still greater splendor and magnificence than at any former period. In 1739, in the height of its prosperity, and when its population was estimated at two millions, it was taken by Nadir Shah. He extorted one hundred and thirty millions of dollars, as a ransom for the city, collected, in jewels and other valuable property, to the amount of two hundred and seventy-five millions, and massacred one hundred and twenty thousand of the inhabitants. Since that time, Delhi has been pillaged and laid waste by other rapacious conquerors, until it has become almost depopulated. The part now inhabited is only seven miles in circuit, while the ruins cover a space much larger than the city of London.

For the purpose of procuring the praise of men and the favor of the gods, Rajahs, and other opulent natives, have, in many of the large towns, built choultries, or inns, for the gratuitous accommodation of travellers. The choultry of Rajah Trimal Naig, at Madura, (see engraving, number 40) consists of one vast hall, three hundred and twelve feet long and one hundred and twenty-five wide. The ceiling is supported by six rows of columns twenty-five feet high. The entire edifice is composed of a hard, gray granite, and every part of its surface is elaborately carved into representations of cows, monkeys, tigers, lions, elephants, men, women, giants, gods, and monsters.

Choultries generally have but one apartment, and are entirely destitute of furniture of every kind. The ground, beaten hard, and covered with lime cement, serves as a floor, which, at night, is strewed with travellers of all classes and of both sexes, wrapped separately in their various-colored cotton cloths, and lying side by side like so many bales of merchandise in a warehouse. As choultries are much of the time unoccupied, they become the favorite resort of bats, monkeys, rats, and serpents. Of these troublesome creatures, the rats are the most annoying, for, while the travellers are asleep, they eat the skin from the soles of their feet, so as often to make it difficult for them to walk for some days afterwards. "I was awoke, and astonished, one night," says a missionary, "by something tugging at my ear. It was a rat. The moment I stirred, my visitant made good his retreat; had my sleep been more sound, I should probably have suffered severely." At another time, as he was sleeping in a choultry, he was awoke by the cry of "Pambu! pambu!"—"A serpent! a serpent!" His bearers were on the alert;—the serpent had passed between them and himself without biting any one. Having ascertained that it was not the cobra, which their superstitious reverence will not allow them to destroy, they killed it, and found it was a species of viper whose bite is fatal. The cobra, and various other reptiles, receive religious homage. Inanimate objects are also deified. Of this numerous class of divinities is the Ganges. The Shasters, which are regarded with as much reverence by the Hindu as the Bible is by the Christian, contain these passages:—

"If a person has been guilty of killing cows* or Brahmins, only let him touch the water of the Ganges, desiring the remis-

* See page 247.

No. 39. *Ruins in Delhi.*

No. 40. Interior of the Great Choultry at Madura.

sion of these sins, and they will immediately be forgiven." And "bathing in the Ganges, accompanied by prayer, will remove all sin." Millions of the Hindus, at a great expense of time, health, and morals, perform pilgrimages to the Ganges. Multitudes travel from five hundred to a thousand miles, and are absent from their home and business five or six months at a time. The Rev. Mr. Thompson, a Baptist missionary, informed me that, on one occasion, he saw more than three hundred thousand pilgrims assembled at Hurdwar, to bathe at the place where Brahma, the creator of the world, is said to have performed his ablutions. At two o'clock in the morning, when it was announced by the Brahmins that the propitious time for the ceremony had arrived, the immense multitude rushed down a flight of steps into the Ganges. Those who first entered the water and bathed, attempted to return, but the passage continued to be wedged up with the dense mass of those who were still descending. There were, indeed, other passages by which they might have returned, but that would not do; it was not the custom. To return by another way would diminish the merit of the bathing. They endeavored, therefore, to force their way upward. Consequently a scene of great violence took place, which resulted in the death of six hundred persons.

Engraving, No. 41 is a view of the junction of the Ganges and Jumna. It is believed that every person, of either sex, who, immediately after being shaved, bathes at the point of land where those two rivers unite, will be permitted to dwell in heaven as many years as the number of hairs removed by the razor. To obtain immediate admission there, many thousands of the pilgrims have drowned themselves here.

The strip of land extending from the point at the junction of the rivers to the Fort of Allahabad, on the right of the engraving, is a desolate waste; but during an annual festival, which I witnessed here, it was crowded with tents, and huts, and more than one hundred thousand pilgrims. On entering this vast encampment, I saw several missionaries, who, in a small shed by the wayside, were preaching the gospel and distributing tracts. A little beyond was the bazaar, or market, where food and various kinds of merchandise were exposed for sale. In a conspicuous place, near the bazaar, was a man seated upon a mat, and surrounded by roots, herbs, lizard-skins, and dried snakes; professing the ability, like the empirics of more enlightened lands, to cure incurable diseases, and set death at defiance. In another part of the encampment were about three hundred religious mendicants.

In the engraving, a barrier or fence is to be seen extending from the Ganges to the Jumna. Soldiers were stationed there, to prevent the pilgrims from passing it, until they had purchased of the East India Company tickets granting permission to bathe. Near the barrier, I saw three devotees, who had held the left arm elevated above the head until it had become immovable, and the finger nails had grown to the length of six or eight inches. A portrait of one of them is to be seen on page 11, of the first lecture. As I approached the point, I saw two or three hundred barbers employed in shaving the heads and bodies of the pilgrims preparatory to bathing. I also witnessed a very shrewd method of getting rid of sin. The person who wished to become perfect took in his right hand some money and a few blades of a particular grass, esteemed sacred. Then, with the same hand, he grasped the tail of a cow, while a Brahmin poured on it some water from the Ganges and repeated an incantation. The money as a matter of course, was given to the Brahmin, the sins were reputed to pass along the tail of the animal, the grass and the deception remained to the pilgrim. Cows were stationed at six or eight places for the convenience of performing this ceremony.

I next visited the point, and found the water, for a considerable distance, crowded with the pilgrims. To bathe at this particular spot was the great object of the pilgrimage.

No. 42 is a sick man, brought to the Ganges to die. His friends have carried him into the sacred stream, and are performing the last fatal rite. It consists in pouring a large quantity of water down his throat; filling his mouth and nostrils with mud; repeating the names of the gods, and shouting, "O mother Ganges, receive his soul!" Thus the sick, instead of receiving medical treatment, kind nursing, and appropriate nourishment, are, in many cases, hurried away to the Ganges, to be purified from their sins, by dying on its banks or in its waters. In Calcutta alone, nineteen hundred sick persons have, in the course of one month, been brought to the Ganges to die. Some are suffocated by filling the mouth and nostrils with mud; others are left where the rising tide will sweep them away.

It is a remarkable fact, that when the sick are brought to the river-side to die, they cannot legally be restored to health. They are regarded by the Hindu law as already dead. Their prop-

No. 41. *Union of the Ganges and Jumna.*

No. 42. *The Sick brought to the Ganges.*

erty passes to their heirs, and in the event of recovery, which sometimes happens, they become outcasts. Their nearest relatives will neither eat with them nor show them the smallest favor. They are held in utter abhorrence, and are allowed to associate only with persons in similar circumstances. I have seen a large village, inhabited entirely by these wretched beings.

Great numbers of the dead are thrown into the Ganges, that their souls may be purified. It has been officially stated that, in the course of one month, more than a thousand human bodies have been seen floating on the surface of the Ganges, in the immediate vicinity of Calcutta. At that place, and as far as its waters are agitated by the tide, it contains so much earthy matter and other impurities, that no object can be seen at the distance of two inches below its surface. Yet the inhabitants of the city use the water of this river for drinking and culinary purposes, and the numerous merchant vessels trading there are supplied with it for the homeward voyage.

Pilgrims carry water from the Ganges into every part of India, to be used for religious and medicinal purposes. It is put up in glass bottles. These are packed in baskets, and suspended from the ends of a bamboo which rests upon the pilgrim's shoulder. I have frequently seen the roads thronged with pilgrims thus accoutred. They resembled an immense army on the march. You will see one of them by turning to the next page of engravings. He has stopped by the wayside, near Balasore, to worship certain stones, an accurate representation of which you see in the engraving. There are his baskets filled with bottles of Ganges water. Having made his *salam*, he mutters a few words in a careless manner, and then takes a bottle of water from one of his baskets, and pours a small quantity of it upon the stones. To appease the wrath, or to procure the favor of divinities like these, splendid festivals are instituted. About ten o'clock at night, the worshippers assemble. By the glare of flaming torches, and amid the shouts and loud peals of barbarous music, great numbers of swine, sheep, goats, and buffaloes, are sacrificed Many of the worshippers throw themselves upon the ground, and wallow in the pools of warm blood flowing from the slaughtered animals. Then, leaping upon their feet, reeking with gore and filth, they jump and frolic, and twist themselves into the most wanton attitudes, and vociferate the most indecent songs, for the gratification of the image, or the rough stone before which these acts of worship are performed.

Number 44 is a scene in the house of a wealthy native, at the celebration of a festival in honor of Ganesa, the god of wisdom. Ganesa is represented as a very corpulent man, of a red color, with four arms, and the head of a white elephant. In front of him is a rat, upon the back of which he is said to perform his journeys. The men on the right are musicians. For the gratification of the idol, and the multitude of assembled worshippers, a dancing girl is performing. She is clad in garments of the finest texture, and of the most brilliant colors, and is decorated with a profusion of costly ornaments. Her movements are slow and monotonous, and occasionally very indecent, and her songs are plentifully spiced with amorous allusions. After singing and dancing for some hours, her place is supplied, either by others of the same class, or by playactors, jugglers, or mountebanks; and the performance is thus continued from ten o'clock till sunrise. Many of the dancing girls belong to the temples, and are called the wives of the gods. At an early age they are united in wedlock to the images worshipped in the temples. This strange matrimonial connection is formed in compliance with the wishes of the parents, who believe it to be a highly meritorious act to present a beautiful daughter, in marriage, to a senseless idol, and thus doom her to a life of vice and infamy. Dancing is deemed so disreputable by the Hindus that none engage in it but the most dissolute and abandoned. Here, as in other countries, there appears to be an intimate connection between dancing and licentiousness.

The following is one of the songs, which, at religious festivals, are sung for the amusement of the idols and their worshippers. The boy mentioned in the first line is Krishna, the favorite divinity, who married sixteen thousand wives. He is believed to have been born of human parents, at Brindabun, on the Ganges, where he spent his youthful days in playing on the flute, and frolicking with the milkmaids.

"The pipe is heard of Nundh's sweet boy —
The milkmaids' hearts beat high with joy;
To the cool woods in crowds they speed;
No danger fear, nor toil, they heed;
And, if by chance the youth they spy,
Away go prudence, modesty.
They gaze, by his bright beauties burned,
And soon their pails are overturned!"

They then go to Jasooda, (Krishna's mother,) and make the following complaint: —

No. 43. *A Pilgrim at his Devotions.*

No. 44. *Ganesa, Dancing Girl, and Musicians.*

"Jasooda! listen to our prayer;
Thy son's audacious frolics hear!
To Brindabun we bent our way;
He seized our arms and bade us stay.
Lady! our cheeks with shame were red;
Like modest girls, away we fled.
In vain we've milked, in vain we've churned,
For he our pails has overturned!"

Jasooda replies,—

"Go, bold and forward milkmaids, go!
No one your wily ways can know;
Often in laughing groups you're seen
Bending your steps to coverts green;
There in the cool retreats you rove,
And pass the hours in mirth and love;
Then tell me, from your pranks returned,
Forsooth, your pails are overturned!"

Extract from one of the Plays performed at Religious Festivals.

KRISHNA.

Again, my fair one!—hast thou purchased me?

MILKMAID.

Think'st thou uncalled I boldly come? Ah, see!—
The gathering clouds, dear youth, invite to love.

KRISHNA.

How could a frame so soft such dangers brave?
While e'en thy pretty self was lost in night
How see thy way?

MILKMAID.

The lightning gleamed so bright.

KRISHNA.

O'er broken roads, through mire and tangling thorn
Thy tender limbs must ache, thy feet be torn.

MILKMAID.

Steps light and firm will weariest way o'ercome.

KRISHNA.

Yet dark's the night, and thou wert all alone.

MILKMAID.

No, my soul's lord! for Love was with me still,
Pointed my path and warded every ill.

No. 45 is the great temple of Juggernaut. The principal edifice rises to the elevation of two hundred feet. In the two adjacent buildings, morning and evening, the dancing girls display their professional skill, for the amusement of the idols enthroned in the large edifice. There, also, three times a day, large quantities of the choicest food are presented to these wooden images. The people are taught that the appetite of these gods is perfectly satisfied by smelling and seeing the food at a distance. This is a remarkably fortunate circumstance, since the Brahmins always take what the idols leave.

The wall which surrounds the temple is about twenty feet high, and forms an enclosure six hundred and fifty feet square. On each side of the square is a gateway. The gateway in the engraving is through the base of a highly-ornamented tower. The small buildings, in front of the wall, are the shops of merchants, where clothing and ornaments are exposed for sale. The column on the right is a very beautiful specimen of architecture. The shaft, which is thirty feet high, is composed of a single stone. The figure on the top is an image of Huneman, a deified monkey.

The only foreigner who ever saw the inside of this temple was an English officer, who, about thirty years since, succeeded in gaining admission, by painting and dressing himself like a native. When the Brahmins discovered that their holy place had been thus defiled, they became so enraged that all the English residing at the station were obliged to flee for their lives. Suspecting their pursuers to be more desirous of gratifying their avarice than their revenge, they strewed silver money by the way, and, while the natives stopped to pick it up, they gained time, and succeeded in reaching a place of safety.

Twelve festivals are annually celebrated here in honor of Juggernaut. The most important of these are the bathing and the car festivals. These I witnessed, and there were present more than one hundred and fifty thousand pilgrims. Nearly half were females. There is not only great suffering among the multitude of pilgrims who, from distant places, attend these festivals, but many of them die in consequence of excessive fatigue, exposure to the annual rains, and the want of suitable and sufficient food. The plains, in many places, are literally whitened with the bones of the pilgrims, while dogs and vultures are continually devouring the bodies of the dead. Rev. Mr. Lacy informed me that, in 1825, he counted ninety dead bodies in one

No. 45. *The Temple of Juggernaut.*

No. 46. *Portrait of Juggernaut*

place, and that his colleague, at the same time, counted one hundred and forty more in another place. Great numbers perish on their way home. The pilgrim, on leaving Puri, has a long journey before him, and his means of support are often almost, if not entirely, exhausted. The rainy season has now commenced, and at every step his naked feet sink deep in the mud. At length, exhausted by hunger and fatigue, he sits down by the side of the road, unable to proceed any farther. His companions, regarding only their own safety, leave him to his fate. Dogs, jackals, and vultures, gather around him, watching his dying struggles; and in a few hours his flesh has disappeared, and his bones lie bleaching on the plain. Since the erection of this temple, in the twelfth century, such has been the fate of millions.

"The old man, faint, just turns aside to rest,
Bethinking he will rise again, refreshed:—
He rises not. Nature can bear no more,—
Exhausted. Ere the setting sun, his bones
Are left to whiten, where the pilgrim died.
Crowds press still onward, heedless of the plaints
From the way-side. No pity from his fellow
(Who soon will drop and groan, as he now groans)
The dying man receives. Forsaken quite,
He gasping lies, far from the holy stream.
The vulture, with raw neck, and fulsome croak,
Claps her smeared wing; she smells, as soaring high,
The riotous feast, and hastens to the spoil.
Hinnom! thou slaughter valley, here behold
Thy counterpart. Not Moloch's self e'er saw
Such carnival of death; drunk with the wine
Of overflowing vintage, lo! he riots
Wantonly; and to mortal view it seems
He throws in random rage the fatal dart
That needs must hit."

No. 46 is a portrait of Juggernaut. I have taken his portrait as I saw him in the morning, while the Brahmins were making his toilet. He appeared to be well supplied with fine Cashmere shawls and valuable jewels, and the Brahmins were so arranging them as to display the beauties of his person to the best advantage. In the evening he is entirely disrobed, and his shawls and jewels, and also his hands and feet, which are made of gold, are carefully locked up in a strong box. This precaution is not through fear that the idol will convey himself away in the night, but to secure these treasures from thieves. Nor is the strong box always a sufficient security, for on one occasion, upon opening it in the morning, jewels to the value of some thousands of dollars had disappeared.

To some, perhaps, it may seem impossible for the human mind to become so debased as to worship an object having no higher claims to homage than this; but, strange as it may seem, this monstrous form has received, and still receives, the adoration of a large portion of the human race.

At one of the annual festivals, Juggernaut and two other images, said to be his brother and sister, are drawn out upon huge cars.

> "Here rolls the hated car,
> Grinding the crashing bones, and hearts, and brains
> Of men and women. Down they fling themselves
> In the deep gash, and wait the heavy wheel
> Slow rolling on its thunder bellowing axle,
> Sunk in the wounded earth. The sigh, the breath,
> The blood, and life, and soul, with spirting rush,
> Beneath the horrid load, forsake the heap
> Of pounded flesh, and the big roar continues
> As though no soul had passed the bounds of time,
> Nor orphans 'gan their wail, no kindly bonds
> Had been dissolved; but the mad living throng,
> Trampling by thousands o'er the dead and dying,
> All nerve and sinew, swelter as they tug,
> And howling, shouting, pulling, hear no groan,
> Nor feel the throes of beings, crushed beneath them.
> The welkin wide is troubled with long peals,
> As though dark demons strode the sultry beams,
> Helping the discord with strange screech or laugh."

No. 47 is the car of Juggernaut. The platform on which the image is placed is thirty-four feet square, and is supported by sixteen wheels, six and a half feet in diameter. The upper part is covered with English broadcloths in alternate stripes of red and yellow. Near the idol is the strong box in which his hands, feet, jewels, and clothing are deposited at night. Six ropes, or cables, are attached to the car, six inches in diameter and three hundred feet in length, by means of which the people draw it from place to place. A devotee has cast himself under the wheels to be crushed to death. As a reward for this act of devotion, he expects to enjoy health, riches, and honors in the next life.

The car festival, which I witnessed at Puri, commenced on the Sabbath. I went to the temple, about two o'clock in the after-

No. 47. *Car of Juggernaut.*

No. 48. *Luckshme, copied from an Ancient Sculpture.*

noon, just as the pilgrims, who had encamped in great numbers in the vicinity, were beginning to assemble. From an elevated position, on an elephant, I saw them pouring in from every direction, until four o'clock, when the concourse became immense. Every street and avenue leading to the temple was thronged, and the flat roofs of the houses were also densely crowded with anxious spectators. About five o'clock, a company of men proceeded from the temple, making a horrid din with drums, gongs, and trumpets. Next came the idols, shaded by umbrellas of state and attended by various emblems of royalty. The vast multitude greeted them with loud and long-continued shouts. Juggernaut, and his brother and sister, were now to mount their cars; but from the infirmities of age, or some more obvious cause, they submitted to the awkward expedient of being dragged through the mud to their elevated seats, by the aid of ropes and Brahmins. A variety of ceremonies followed, but, as it was growing late, I returned to my lodgings.

At sunrise the next morning, the gates of the town were thrown open, to admit the beggars. As they passed, I was informed by the English magistrate, by whose order they were admitted, that their number probably exceeded fifty thousand. They were the most weary, ragged, filthy, wretched-looking objects I ever saw. They had been prevented from entering the town at an earlier period, because of their inability to pay the tax which the *Honorable* East India Company demanded of their heathen subjects for the privilege of seeing their idols. The Company, I ascertained, had,. in the preceding thirty-four days, received fifty-five thousand dollars as admission fees. Having already extorted so large a sum from the richer pilgrims, they could well afford, now that a part of the festival was over, to admit gratuitously those from whom no money could be extorted. It affords me much pleasure to say that this unrighteous source of gain has recently been abolished. The multitude of beggar pilgrims hastened onward to the cars, and appeared to be lost in the much larger multitude there assembled.

Hearing the tumultuous sound of many voices at a distance, I looked towards the place from which it came, when I saw about a thousand men advancing, with green branches elevated in their hands. They rushed forward, leaping through the crowd, and, with mighty shoutings, seized the ropes of one of the cars, and dragged it forth in triumph. Soon other companies, in a similar manner, dashed forward and put the two remaining cars in motion.

The pilgrims are taught to believe that the cars are not moved and guided by the strength of the men who pull at the ropes, but by the will and pleasure of the idols. This being admitted, it must be that Juggernaut made a grand mistake, for he ran his car against a house, and was not able to extricate himself until the afternoon of the next day. But perhaps he was merely in a surly mood, for they believe that the cars move only when the idols are pleased with the worship. So, if for any reason a car stops, they suppose that the idol thus expresses his disapprobation. One of the priests then steps forward to the front of the platform, as here represented, rehearses the deeds and extols the character of the idol, in a manner the most obscene. No person, educated in a Christian country, can possibly conceive expressions so debasing and abominable as are used on such occasions. Should the speaker quote from the Shasters, or invent an expression more than usually lascivious, the multitude give a shout, or rather a sensual yell. The men again pull, with renewed energy, at the ropes, the idol is supposed to be delighted, and the car is permitted to move on. When dragged a short distance farther, it is stopped again by a priest, who slyly clogs one of the wheels. Then another scene of pollution is acted out with all its debasing influence upon the mind and morals of the people. In this manner, eight days are spent in drawing the car about two miles.

In one of the apartments of Juggernaut's temple, there is a golden image of Luckshme, the wife of Juggernaut. Near midnight, on the fourth day of the car festival, it was brought out of the temple, on a splendid litter, borne on the shoulders of men. Preceded by a band of rude music, and men bearing flaming torches, they soon approached the cars, when Luckshme was presented directly in front of Juggernaut, her husband. Immediately the whole multitude appeared to be in a perfect rage, and rent the air with the most violent and clamorous yells. The women, who at this time were unusually numerous, appeared to be by far the most excited. In the midst of these dreadful yells, which had now continued several minutes, one of the priests took a garland of flowers from Juggernaut, and placed it around the neck of his wife. She was then borne off towards the temple, and the clamor ceased.

I inquired the meaning of this strange and terrific ceremony. The reply was, that on the first day of the festival, Juggernaut had eloped with his sister. That, on the fourth, his wife heard of

No. 49. A CEREMONY AT THE TEMPLE OF JUGGERNAUT.

Krishna, accompanied by two other images, is brought out of the temple and suspended from a lofty stone arch, very curiously wrought. He is then swung by the Brahmins for his gratification, and the amusement of the worshippers. *See page 98.*

it, and, being stung with jealousy, determined on revenge. Accordingly, she set out in hot pursuit of her unfaithful spouse; and, having overtaken him at this place, she had given him a sound scolding. The shouting and yelling of the multitude was merely the effect of sympathy, they joining in the chorus with the scolding wife. This accounts for the active part which the women took in this ceremony. Juggernaut, like other penitent husbands who have scolding wives, promises to do better in future, and Luckshme is persuaded to be reconciled and to return home.

You will readily perceive that this festival exerts a most pernicious influence upon the community. The ceremonies are not only foolish, but most polluting in their tendencies and effects. Here crimes of the foulest character are sanctioned by the conduct of their supreme god. It is not, therefore, a matter of sur prise that impurity, and all its kindred abominations, pervade the land. Let us, who live in this Christian country, thank God for the revelation of his own glorious character; and while we bless him for the Bible, and for all those spiritual influences which have made us to differ from the heathen, shall we not strive to send them the gospel? Freely we have received; freely let us give.

Engraving, No. 50 is a view near the city of Benares. The building at the right of the ghat, or flight of steps, is a temple of Shiva. The one on the left is a resting-place for pilgrims. The water is in a tank about two hundred feet square. In November, about one hundred thousand persons assemble around this tank, to perform a variety of ceremonies for the benefit of the souls of deceased relatives.

The pepul-trees, in the engraving, are supposed to be the favorite resort of such departed spirits as, from various causes, have not yet been clothed with new bodies. While I was engaged in taking a drawing of this place, several of the natives came and put lighted lamps in the earthen pots which you see suspended from the branches of the trees. On inquiring of one why he did so, he replied, "That the soul of my relative may be in light." I asked him how he knew whether the soul of his relative was in darkness or light. He said, "It is impossible for me to know that. But it is our custom, when one of the family dies, to suspend an earthen pot from a pepul-tree, and for ten successive days to bring offerings of water and rice, with a lighted lamp, for the benefit of the departed. On the tenth day, we break the pot, and make a feast for the Brahmins." In Calcutta, I witnessed a feast of this character, made by a wealthy merchant for the benefit of his deceased mother. The number of guests was estimated at two hundred thousand, and the expense of the feast, together with the presents made, was estimated at seventy-five thousand dollars.

The efficacy of one of the numerous ceremonies for the benefit of deceased relatives is supposed to depend very much upon the place where it is performed. If performed at a certain temple in the town of Guyah, it is supposed that inconceivable benefits will be conferred upon the deceased. The East India Company, seizing upon this superstitious feeling, have until recently made it a source of revenue by imposing a tax upon all who perform this ceremony at Guyah. The tax collected at that temple amounted to about one hundred and twelve thousand dollars annually.

Ceremonies for the repose of the soul are exceedingly numerous; but I will mention only one more. The son of the deceased procures one male and four female calves. These are tied to five posts, near an altar, constructed for the occasion. Four learned Brahmins sit on the four sides of the altar, and offer a burnt sacrifice. A fifth Brahmin reads certain passages in the Shasters, to drive away evil spirits. The son washes the tail of the male calf, and with the same water presents a drink-offering to his deceased ancestors. The male and the four female calves are then gravely united in wedlock. During the marriage ceremony, many formulas are repeated, in which the parties are recommended to cultivate love and mutual sympathy. The Brahmins, having performed the duties of their sacred office, are dismissed with presents, including the four brides; but the bridegroom is dedicated to Shiva, and allowed to run at large until old age carries him off. These vagrant calves may almost be said to constitute one of the numerous orders of religious mendicants, or holy beggars. As no provision is made for their daily wants, and as they are under the necessity of securing their living, they become very cunning, and are scarcely less impudent than the bipeds constituting the other orders of that fraternity. It is not uncommon for them to walk up, unbidden, to the stalls where vegetables are for sale, and help themselves. Being esteemed sacred, the poor deluded inhabitants dare to use only the most gentle means of ridding themselves of their unprofitable customers. During the first year or two, these cattle fare rather scantily; but, after having learned their sacred functions, they live well, and are the fattest and best-looking of all the animals to be seen in Hindustan.

No. 50. *View in Benares.*

No. 51. *The India Ox.*

The Shasters teach that the souls of the departed are divided into five classes. Those of the first class reunite with Brahm, the Eternal Spirit, and thus lose their individuality. The second are admitted to the various heavens of the gods. The third are punished in places of torment. The fourth again become the offspring of human parents. The fifth become beasts, birds, and insects. Hence, should a Hindu inhale an insect with his breath, he knows not but, in so doing, he has swallowed some departed relative — possibly his own father. There is one sect, who, to prevent so horrid a catastrophe, wear a strainer over the mouth.

Hinduism leads its votaries into the wildest and most absurd vagaries in regard to omens, dreams, visions, evil spirits, and witches. In the vicinity of Puna, a person dreamed that the cholera, then raging in his village, was inflicted by a certain woman commissioned by Zurremurre, the goddess of the cholera. The villagers, on hearing this, immediately assembled and put her to death. In Orissa, a woman was told by her priest that Kali, the goddess whom she worshipped, had appeared to him in a vision, and had commanded him to inform her that she must sacrifice her only child. In the night, while he slept, she cut off his head, and gave it to the priest as an offering to the idol. In Nagpore, several persons died suddenly, which led many to believe that they had been destroyed by witchcraft. They therefore employed a man, who professed to be skilled in the art of magic, to discover the authors of their death. He put some oil and rice into a leaf, and began to repeat the name of each person belonging to the village. When he called the name of a certain woman, the oil, as he said, ran through the leaf. This circumstance was regarded as sufficient proof of her guilt. She was immediately seized, and whipped until death ended her sufferings. The death of the favorite wife of Rajah Zelim Singh, of Kotah, being attributed to witchcraft, he sentenced four hundred women to be put into sacks and thrown into a tank. It is stated by General Malcolm, in an official report, that, in the province of Malwa alone, in the course of thirty years, between two and three thousand females had been put to death for the imputed crime of witchcraft.

Many of the Hindus believe that those persons who commit suicide become malignant spirits delighting in every kind of mischief.

The scene represented by engraving No. 53 occurred in Ghazepore. A man persuaded his wife to permit him to burn her alive, that her soul might be transformed into an evil spirit, for the purpose of haunting and tormenting one of their neighbors, who had offended them. In Calcutta, a servant, having quarrelled with his master, hung himself, in the night, in front of the street door, that he might become a devil and haunt the premises. The house was immediately forsaken by its occupants, and, though a large and beautiful edifice, suffered to go to ruin.

In Mirzapoor, a Brahmin took his own child, an infant about fifteen months old, from the arms of its mother, and, holding it by the legs, dashed its head against the ground, that it might become an evil spirit and torment a certain person by whom he imagined himself injured. Another little girl was, by her own father, beheaded with an axe. Another was stabbed to the heart, with a dagger, and her bleeding body thrown at the door of the person upon whom the murderer sought to be revenged. I could give the particulars of many other murders which have been committed for similar purposes.

"Among the customs of the Hindus, there is one which is called *Dherna*. If a man demands satisfaction from his neighbor for some grievous offence, — if a creditor determines to pursue extreme measures with his debtor, to obtain what is due to him, — if a relative has been cheated by another out of his patrimony or his rights, and wishes to exact them from him, — they respectively take the poniard or a cup of poison in their hand, and, knowing that the offending party is at home, they sit down at his door, in dherna. That moment the defendant within is considered as under arrest. He cannot touch food, so long as his accuser continues to fast; and, should he not come to terms, but drive, by his obstinacy, the plaintiff to despair, and allow him to use the dagger or drink the poison, his blood rests upon his head. This may be termed their *ordeal* — their mode of demanding satisfaction — their system of duelling — their *dernier resort*.

"At the village of Pannabaka, in the presidency of Madras, there was a priestly Brahmin, who had lately come from Bellary, and had undertaken to attend upon the idol of the place. His was the privilege to levy contributions on the inhabitants for his sup-

No. 52. *A Devotee leaping from a precipice.*

No. 53. *A man burning his wife alive.*

port. A householder, who had for a time given him a halfpenny a day, refused to continue his allowance; and, though the priest insisted upon the payment, he remained inflexible. The priest then threatened that, unless he received the amount, he would cut out his own tongue, and the householder would have to answer for giving him such a provocation. Incensed at the obstinacy of his opponent, he whetted his knife and cut off the tip of his tongue. He bled profusely, and his tongue swelled to a prodigious size. The pains which he endured only served to render him more desperate, and he declared he would bring his whole family and sit in dherna, till he should obtain a sum sufficient to make a feast to his god. The householder was not to be intimidated, and remained as obstinate as the Brahmin. The priest, his wife, and his four sons, sat down, and kept their position at the door of the defendant; but, during the second night, the female was bit by a snake, and died in the morning. This event exasperated the priest; he increased his demand; and, as the village had remained neutral in the affair, he now laid a tax upon all its inhabitants. As he had not only sustained a personal injury, but had lost his wife while standing up for the rights of his order, and for the honor of his god, nothing less would satisfy him now, than a sum adequate to meet the expenses of the funeral and to make a feast to propitiate the deity who was offended by such daring sacrilege. Till these demands were met, he resolved to keep his station, and to retain the corpse of his wife unburied at the door of the house. As the people of the village rejected his claim, he then threatened that, in order to be avenged upon them, he would first kill his four children, and then put an end to his own existence. It was the act of a Brahmin; it might be viewed by Hindus as a pardonable offence; it was done in honor of his god; it was occasioned by the obstinacy of the people; it was a sacrifice that, according to a monstrous mythology, would meet with a future and a bountiful reward; its helpless victims were to be raised to life again by the divinity whose honor it was done to vindicate. But it is not ours to make apologies; we have only to record the fact, that this priest — this worshipper of Shiva — this monster — this raging fury — took his knife, laid hold of three of his children, and severed their heads from their bodies. It was not enough! His eldest son tried to make his escape; but this murderous father allured him back, and promised that, prior to his own self-destruction, he only wished to embrace him and bid him farewell. Thus invited back by the soft whispers of love, he returned; but, the moment that he came within the grasp of the murderer, he laid him prostrate, as another victim at the shrine of superstition and revenge. His attempt to despatch himself ended in making a dreadful wound in the back of his neck.

"Such, it may be said, are only solitary instances. It would not be right to quote such deeds to bring opprobrium upon a whole people, any more than it would be just to appeal to the horrid murders in Christian countries as a specimen of our own customs. But the cases are utterly dissimilar. The inhabitants of Pannabaka stood by and saw the horrid deed performed; they seemed, afterwards, to be amused and highly delighted at the bravery of the act; they expressed their resentment at one individual, and at the police-officer, who called upon them to interfere to prevent it; and there can be no question that, if this priest had been restored to his liberty and his horrid altar again, they would have received him with enthusiasm, and revered him as a saint of superior sanctity. In a village some miles distant from the spot, the people no sooner heard of this murder, than they left their employment and proceeded to Pannabaka with every demonstration of joy; and, after a few days, they returned, saying, 'The children are not indeed restored to life; but why are they not? It is entirely owing to the inhabitants, who have not made a feast,' which would cost two thousand rupees, to propitiate the favor of the god — a feast which the priest had declared to be necessary." —

On a certain occasion, the Bhats of Marwar demanded a favor of Umra I., and, being refused, determined to sit in dherna. They assembled, with their women and children, in the court of the royal palace, and, with their daggers, commenced a horrid butchery. Eighty of their number lay weltering in their blood.

No. 54 is a group of women engaged in various occupations. One is smoking tobacco. Another is spinning cotton. A third is preparing the thread for the weavers by winding it on a spool. A fourth is preparing the cotton for spinning. A fifth is grinding, upon a flat stone, cayenne pepper, garlic, ginger, and turmeric. These, when stewed with a cucumber or melon, serve as a seasoning for their boiled rice, which, in many parts of India, constitutes more than seven eighths of the entire food of the inhabitants. The woman with the large brass pot is carrying home water for household use. The next is returning from her morning ablution in the Ganges, with her hair spread upon her shoulders to dry

No. 54. *A Group of Women.*

No 55. *Interior of a Dwelling.*

In her left hand are two brass pots, which she has scoured by rubbing them with the mud of the river. Children are never carried in the arms; they sit astride on the hip. The woman carrying the child is going to market with a bundle of wood borne upon the head.

Perhaps there is no one point in which Christianity has a more direct influence upon the state of the community than in respect to the character and standing of the female. To a Hindu the birth of a daughter is an occasion of sorrow. At the early age of twelve or thirteen years, she is required to leave the parental roof, and to become the wife of a man whom she has had no voice in choosing as her companion. Her duties to him are thus prescribed in the Shasters: "When in the presence of her husband, a woman must keep her eyes upon her master, and be ready to receive his commands. When he speaks, she must be quiet, and listen to nothing beside. When he calls, she must leave every thing else, and attend upon him alone. A woman has no other god on earth than her husband. The most excellent of all good works she can perform is, to gratify him with the strictest obedience. This should be her only devotion. Though he be aged, infirm, dissipated, a drunkard, or a debauchee, she must still regard him as her god. She must serve him with all her might, obeying him in all things, spying no defects in his character, and giving him no cause for disquiet. If he laughs, she must also laugh; if he weeps, she must also weep; if he sings, she must be in an ecstasy. She must never eat until her husband is satisfied. If he abstains, she must also fast; and she must abstain from whatever food her husband dislikes."

In engraving, No. 55 you will see the interior of a Hindu dwelling at meal time. The husband, according to custom, is seated upon a mat, eating his boiled rice with his fingers, while his wife is standing by him ready to obey his commands. She is never permitted to eat with her husband, but waits upon him in the capacity of a servant, and afterwards partakes of the fragments in retirement.

Schools are not uncommon in India, but there are none for the instruction of the female. Her mind is entirely uncultivated, and she has no fixed principles to regulate her conduct. She is therefore an easy prey to vice, and the devoted slave of superstition. When her husband dies, she must either burn herself upon his funeral pile, or, if she determines to live, it must be a life of reproach and servitude. She may never marry again, however young she may be. She must cast off all her ornaments, shave her head, and either become a servant in the house of her husband's friends, or adopt a mode of life which will bring disgrace not only upon herself, but upon the whole family. Hence it is, that death upon the funeral pile is so often preferred to surviving widowhood. This cruel custom was, in 1827, prohibited by the East India Company in their own dominions; but in some of the independent provinces the practice is still continued.

A large proportion of the persons who undertake long and hazardous pilgrimages, and who subject themselves to painful modes of self-torture, are females. "At a certain time," says a missionary of my acquaintance, "as I was walking in a retired village, my attention was arrested by seeing two objects, at some distance before me, rolling in the mud. As I approached the spot, I found two females, almost exhausted by fatigue. I learnt that they had vowed to their goddess to roll, in this manner, from one temple to another. They had spent nearly the whole day, and had not accomplished one half their journey. But no arguments, no remonstrances, on my part, could induce them to relinquish their undertaking; for they feared that, unless they performed their vow, the goddess would be angry with them. On leaving these deluded votaries of superstition," continued he, "with my feelings aroused almost to indignation, I expostulated with a learned Brahmin who stood not far distant, and pointed to the miserable objects I had just left. 'O,' said he, 'this is worship exactly suited to the capacity of females. Let them alone They are sincere: of course their worship will be accepted.'"

I might relate many other facts to show the wretched condition of women in pagan lands, but these must suffice. The respected ladies of this audience will permit me to say, in conclusion, every thing in life, in death, and eternity, that can inspire you with the love of existence, you derive from the gospel. To you, then, in a special manner, is the gospel "glad tidings of great joy."

No. 56. *Saugor Island.*

This island is inhabited only by wild beasts. Here thousands of Hindu mothers have thrown their children into the Gangas to be devoured by alligators.

No. 57. *The Bannian Tree.*

" Branching so broad and long, that in the ground
The bending twigs take root; and daughters grow
About the mother tree; a pillared shade,
High overarched, with echoing walks between."

LECTURE

ON THE

CONDITION OF WOMEN IN INDIA,

AND OTHER

PAGAN AND MOHAMMEDAN COUNTRIES.

Woman, in her original state, (to use the language of another,) "was all that is lovely in form, all that is graceful in manner, all that is exalted in mind, all that is pure in thought, all that is delicate in sentiment, all that is enchanting in conversation." She was God's most finished workmanship. Has she lost her original purity and loveliness? But man has fallen too; and relatively they are to each other still what they were before they took and ate of the forbidden fruit. It is now, as ever, Heaven's will that woman receive all "due benevolence" from man,—that he regard her as his equal, and entitled to his warmest love: that he throw his arm around her for protection, and combine with the gentlest care the most respectful deference to her honor and her happiness. "A man shall leave his father and his mother and cleave unto his wife, and they shall be one flesh." "Husbands, love your wives," is God's command and nature's law, for they are bone of each other's bone and flesh of each other's flesh. SUCH IS THE GENIUS OF CHRISTIANITY. And the result of obedience to this eternal law of God and nature, is the lofty elevation of the female character, the thorough cultivation of her mind, the rich endowment of her heart, and the augmented strength of all her capabilities of usefulness and enjoyment; while the result of disobedience is fraught with all that is degrading to intellect, vitiating to social principle, corrupting to moral habits, and hostile to every upward movement of the immortal powers.

And what is the spirit of heathenism, and of false religion in its varied forms, let the impartial pen of history tell. Times, ancient and modern,—witnesses, Pagan, Mahometan, and Christian, may be indiscriminately cited on this point. Their testimony is one,—truthful, melancholy, and decisive.

A daughter is born. 'T is a grievous calamity. The Hindu father becomes dejected, and his neighbors gather around him to mingle their grief with his. The Chinese parent thus afflicted denominates the little innocent a *woo*, a hated thing. Even the Moorish mother repines, and though she had rejoiced greatly at the birth of her son, and blackened her face forty days in token of her joy, yet when a daughter comes into the world, she ill conceals her mortification, by blackening half her face, for half the period only.

It was not long since, that the lady of a missionary in the East, having become the mother of a lovely daughter, a native friend of the husband called on him the following day with a countenance unusually sad. The missionary kindly inquired the cause of his sadness. His friend, with most lugubrious face, replied, "I have heard that your new-born infant is a daughter, and I have come to condole with you, on your hard fate." So little valued is the life of female infants, within the domains of Paganism, that great numbers are put to death, solely to avoid the trouble and expense of feeding and clothing them.

The singular custom formerly prevailed in the northern part of Hindustan, whenever a female child was born, of carrying her to the market-place, and there, holding up the child in one hand, and a knife in the other, proclaiming, that if any person wanted to rear her for a wife, they might then take her; if none appeared to accept of her, she was immediately destroyed. The consequence of this course, was, that the men of the tribe became much more numerous than the women; and hence arose the custom of appropriating several husbands to one wife,—a custom that still prevails in some of the southern as well as the northern tribes of Hindustan. Among the Rajpoot tribes in the north-west part of that country nearly all the female children are put to death immediately after birth; consequently the men are obliged to procure their wives from other tribes. And among some, at least, of the Indian tribes of our own land, the case is no better. Said a Chippewa Indian, (in a recent address before a missionary society in London,)—"When a boy is born in the tribe it is a day of rejoicing, because it is considered that he will make a fine warrior; but when a female is born, it is a time of sorrow and it is said, 'a good-for-nothing girl is born.' The poor mother, knowing that the news is not good, kisses the poor child, and

Three Hindu Girls — Anna, Rajee and Rabee. They were educated at the Orphan Girls School at Burdwan.

says, 'Father does not love you, but I do;' and then, taking the infant by the legs, dashes out its brains, exclaiming, 'Would to God, my mother had done so with me when I was born,—I should not then have been such a slave.' On one occasion the helpless babe was rescued from its mother, by her sisters, who said, 'It is better that your child should be a slave than to kill it in this way.' That babe is now grown up; when fourteen years of age, she was converted, and has now become a Sabbath school teacher, and a useful member of society."

THE EDUCATION OF HEATHEN FEMALES IS ENTIRELY NEGLECTED. While, throughout the Eastern world, schools are maintained for the instruction of boys, and they are sufficiently taught to qualify them for the common business of life, girls are left to utter ignorance of letters, and systematically refused all intellectual culture, as useless to themselves and injurious to society. To a European gentleman, (who endeavored to persuade the natives of a Hindu village that the education of their females in reading, writing, and arithmetic, would be of advantage to their husbands, and would render them their equals and companions, as well as helpers,) it was replied,—"All this, Sahib, may be very true with your people, but it will never do for us. It would be impossible for Hindus to keep their wives in subjection, if they were educated." Shrewd reasoning this!—based on the preposterous assumption, that man is created to be a master, and woman a slave. In vain were these villagers assured that women of the most refined education and extensive knowledge are the most affectionate and faithful wives in the world, because governed by reason, judgment, and common sense, they regard the interest of their husbands as their own, and yield a systematic and cheerful obedience in those things in which the husband's will ought to have the preference, while, at the same time, he might enjoy the advantages of her better judgment in matters which pertain to her own sphere. Their only reply to such arguments is, "Our women are not like yours,—if educated they would be refractory, and would no longer carry burdens, and collect cow's ordure for fuel." On grounds like these, is the whole mass of female mind throughout Hindustan, China, Burmah, Persia, Turkey, &c., doomed to perpetual darkness and gloom, instead of sharing the light of science, and rejoicing in the radiance of the sun of righteousness.

THEY ARE NOT AT THEIR OWN DISPOSAL IN MARRIAGE. Of all the relationships of life, this is the basis. Of all affinities, it is the closest and most tender. Of earthly bliss, it is the purest fountain,—the brightest crown,—the loveliest image of heaven's blest communion.

> "True bliss (if man may reach it) is composed
> Of hearts in union mutually disclosed;
> And farewell else, all hope of pure delight."

"In marriage," (says Jeremy Taylor,) "kindness is spread abroad, and love is united, and made firm as a centre; it is the nursery of heaven,—it fills up the number of the elect. It is the mother of the world, and preserves the kingdoms, and fills the cities, and the churches, and heaven itself. Like the useful bee, it builds a house, and gathers sweetness from every flower, and labors, and unites into societies and republics, and sends out colonies, and feeds the world with delicacies, and keeps order, and promotes the interest of mankind, and is that state of good things, to which God has designed the present constitution of the world."

But all this supposes confidence and esteem, growing out of acquaintance between the parties,—affection, inspiring a mutual desire to please, and the immerging of individual interests in the common stock of domestic enjoyments. And of this, Paganism knows nothing. It holds females as articles of merchandise, to be disposed of to those who will pay for them the highest price. Girls of six or eight years are bought and sold by their fathers as calves of the stall, to be taken, at twelve or fourteen, (whether willing or unwilling,) from the home of their childhood, and put into the hands of the man for whom they were purchased.

In Hindustan, females, who remain unmarried till they are fifteen or sixteen years of age, (however correct in their conduct,) are regarded as infamous, and (like widows) are never sought for in marriage; and widowers (even if sixty or seventy years old) invariably marry girls of ten or twelve. Among the poorer classes in China, when a man dies, his relatives (to regain the money originally paid for his bride) are allowed to sell his widow to become the wife of another man. The arrangement is made without her knowledge, and (regardless of her wishes) she is forced into a palenkeen, and carried to the house of her purchaser. The price of a bride varies much in different countries. In some parts of Africa ten or fifteen bullocks are paid as an equivalent, while a handsome red-haired Circassian or Georgian girl cannot be bought for less than six or seven thousand piasters. In the kingdom of Dahomey, all unmarried women are held as the property of the king. Once a year they assemble at the

Women of Calcutta.

palace, when he selects the handsomest for himself, and sells the remainder to his subjects. The purchaser is allowed no choice, but receives the wife selected for him by the king. But the whole story of man's regard for woman in unevangelized lands, is told in the simple language of the Modean of Siberia, who, at the close of the marriage ceremony, places the bride on a mat, and conveys her to the bridegroom, saying, "There, wolf, take thy lamb."

It is not in all heathen countries, however, that wives are obtained by money or its equivalent. In some tribes more romantic customs prevail. The New Hollander fixes his eye upon some female of a tribe at enmity with his own. He steals upon her at some moment when no protector is near, and deals out blows with his club, upon her head, neck, back, indeed every part of her body, till she becomes insensible; and then drags her by one of her arms, (the blood streaming from her wounds,) over rocks, hills, stones and logs, with all the violence and ferocity of a savage, till he reaches his tribe. The scene that follows, admits not of description. Suffice it to say, the poor violated woman becomes the wife of her ravisher,—is admitted to his tribe,—and (notwithstanding the singularity of the courtship) is contented with her lot, and rarely leaves her husband and her home.

That genuine love may exist, even among these rude barbarians, and sometimes be exhibited in the purest forms, admits not of doubt. Mr. Barrington (who had long resided in Parametta) mentions an instance that fell under his own observation, pleasantly illustrating this fact. "A brother of twenty-three, and two sisters of twenty and fourteen respectively, dwelt together affectionately in a cave near the city. On returning one day from hunting the kangaroo, just as the darkness of night mantled the heavens, and while the forked lightning played vividly around him, at the mouth of the cave, his eye caught the form of his younger sister, bleeding on the ground. Troubled before at the warring of the elements, his soul was now in agony. He endeavored to raise her up, but she was senseless. At length, however, his efforts were successful, and, with returning animation, she exclaimed, 'Dear brother! our sister is torn from us,—a wretch came to the cave, beat her cruelly with his club, and caught up one arm to drag her away,—I laid hold of the other to prevent him, but the moment he saw it, with a single blow, he knocked me to the ground, where you have now found me.' The night was passed in the anguish of grief and amid harrowing purposes of revenge. Morning came. Together they sought the tribe of the offender. A little before reaching it, they met the sister of the very man who had committed the outrage, gathering sticks for a fire. A fine opportunity was thus presented for revenge. The brother (bidding his sister to hide herself) flew upon the young woman, with club in hand, and with all the ferocity of a savage in his heart. The victim trembled; but knowing his power, she stood firmly, and looked him in the eye, when, (like the lion of the forest, meeting the eye of intelligent man,) he paused,—he gazed,—enchantment was on him: she saw it,—dropped on her knees and implored his compassion. Revenge softened into love; throwing down his club, he clasped her in his arms, and vowed eternal constancy. This nobleness won her heart. He called his sister, who thirsted still for the stranger's blood, and said to her, 'She is now my wife.'"

> "Nor force nor interest joined unwilling hands,
> But love consenting tied the blissful bands."

All three now love each other tenderly, and (under the instruction of a Christian friend) read the oracles of God, and cherish the spirit that breathes from the bosom of Jesus.

Polygamy prevents the enjoyment of the husband's affection. Conjugal love may be disturbed,—or it may be diminished,—or it may be maddened into phrensy,—or it may be annihilated,—but it cannot be divided. Abraham may become the husband of Hagar, but his heart is with Sarah. Jacob may be the protector of Leah, but he loves Rachel. Elkanah may deal kindly with Peninnah, but his affections are with Hannah. Good men these, and faithful to their marriage-vows, though borne away into the transgression of the original law of Heaven, by the strong current of the popular sentiment of the age in which they lived. Then, though Heaven interfered not to prevent the practice, it never sanctioned it by law; and if it were not condemned by statutes and penalties, it was powerfully rebuked by its effects and consequences. Never did it fail, in the most auspicious circumstances for its indulgence, to produce domestic discord and wretchedness. Jealousy, bitterness, and strife, are its invariable attendants, even when associated with faith as strong as that of the patriarchs, and piety as ardent as that of the sweet singer of Israel. Its inconsistency with the spirit of the gospel has expelled the practice from every Christian land; and its incongruity with reason and expediency, has stamped it with infamy. But it still prevails among the higher classes, in nearly every part of the unevangelized world.

A Hindu Woman of Bengal, of high rank, in full Dress.

Besides four queens, the king of Birmah has thirty wives, and five hundred other women at his disposal. The emperor of Turkey swells his harem, usually, with more than a thousand wives,—the sultan Achmet I. is said to have had three thousand. The king of Ashantee has three thousand three hundred and thirty-three,—a mystical number, on the integrity of which the prosperity of his kingdom is supposed to depend. And the king of Yarriba boasted to Capt. Clapperton, that his wives, linked hand in hand, would reach entirely across his kingdom.

Not only kings, but nobles, and men of wealth and station, and indeed men of all classes, who have the ability to sustain a plurality of wives, are eager to possess them,—not as objects of affection, but as honorable appendages to their establishments, or as ministering to their pride and sensuality. Love is not known

> ——— "where pleasure is adored,
> That ruling goddess, with a zoneless waist
> And wandering eyes, still leaning on the arm
> Of novelty."

but its place is supplied by envy, and rancor, and hate, bursting forth, often, in words of wrath and deeds of cruelty, and the wanton murder of the innocent. Says Lady Montague, during her residence in Constantinople, "The body of a young woman of surpassing beauty was found one morning near my house. She had received two wounds, one in her side, and the other in her breast, and was not quite cold. Many came to admire her beauty; but no one could tell who she was,—no woman's face being known out of her family. She was buried privately, and little inquiry made for the wretch who had imbrued his hands in her blood." The Pacha of Acre, in Palestine, a few years since, put to death seven of his wives, at one time, with his own hands. And even where cruelties like these are not perpetrated, the wife is kept a prisoner in the house of her lord, and her face is never seen beyond it. She is thus entirely in the irresponsible power of her husband, nor is one earthly ear but his, open to the tale of her wrongs, how terrible soever they may be. That she endures such wrongs, is no more to be questioned than the existence of caprice in man's proud heart, or of contempt for the whole sex, which he regards as infinitely inferior to his own.

The Pagan or Mahometan wife is liable to divorce, and consequent poverty and shame, at any moment when her husband wills it. For one cause, and only one, Christianity permits the disruption of the conjugal tie. And it is this inviolability of the relation that operates so kindly in the restraint of unseemly passions, and in perpetuating

> "Domestic happiness, the only bliss
> Of Paradise that has survived the fall."

But false religions allow to man unbounded license. Might and right, in their vocabulary, are but synonymous terms; and woman (dishonored without her own fault) is, at her husband's pleasure, turned an outcast from her home. Let the Arab's wife be taken sick, and forthwith she is returned to her parents with the message, "I paid for a healthy woman, and cannot afford the support of a sickly one." Let the Siberian become dissatisfied with his wife, for any cause, and he has but to tear her cap from her head, and the marriage contract is dissolved. Let the husband of Sumatra but break a bamboo, in the presence of his wife and their relatives, and the divorce is effected. Or, let the Greenlander leave his home in apparent anger, and not return for a few days; the wife understands his meaning, picks up her clothes, and returns to her friends. Or let the South Sea Islander but speak the word, and the relation is dissolved, though no dislike of the wife to the husband can produce a separation without his consent. But a divorce is ruin to the female,—it dooms her irrevocably to scorn and universal contempt, and (with scarcely less certainty) to a life of vice and infamy.

But the degradation of woman under the fell influence of false religions is not yet fully seen. She is her husband's slave, and with unquestioning servility, must yield to his behest, on penalty of torture, separation, or death. Nor is this a mere accident of her condition. The religion of her country decrees it,—the sacred books demand it. The Koran, and the Hindu Shasters, whose doctrines sway the mind, and determine the practice, of more than two hundred millions of the human family, make woman infinitely man's inferior,—the mere pander to his passions,—the abject drudge, owing him unconditional submission. Says the Shaster of the Hindu,—"The supreme duty of a wife, is, to obey the mandate of her husband. Let the wife who wishes to perform sacred ablution, wash the feet of her lord, and drink the water, for the husband is to the wife greater than Vishnoo. If a man goes on a journey his wife shall not divert herself by play, nor shall see any public show, nor shall laugh, nor shall dress herself in jewels and fine clothes, nor shall see dancing, nor hear music, nor shall sit at the window, nor shall ride out, nor shall behold anything choice and rare, but shall facten well the house door, and remain private, and shall not eat any dainty food, and

A Mohammedan Woman of Bengal, of high rank, in full Dress

shall not blacken her eyes with powder, and shall not view her face in a mirror,—she shall never exercise herself in any such agreeable employment during the absence of her husband." Again, "A woman shall never go out of the house without the consent of her husband, and shall act according to the orders of her husband, and shall not eat until she has served him,"—though, "if it be physic, she may take it before he eat."

Not only in Hindustan, but in almost every unevangelized country, the wife is obliged to stand and wait upon her husband while he eats, and to be content with such food as is left after his wants are satisfied. In the Society Islands, while Paganism reigned, women were not only thus compelled to wait upon their husband's table, but were not allowed, on pain of death, to eat at all of those kinds of food which were most highly esteemed. The cocoa-nut, the plantain, the fowl, the turtle, the swine, the shark, and various kinds of fish, were tabued to them. Nor were they allowed to eat in the same house with the men, nor to cook their food at the same fire, nor to put it into the same vessels. The transgression of these rules involved immediate drowning or strangulation. "The females of Raratonga," (says the Rev. Mr. Williams,) "were denied those kinds of food reserved for the men and the gods,—compelled to eat their scanty meals by themselves, and forbidden to dwell under the same roof with their tyrannical masters."

Till Riho Riho became ruler of the Sandwich Islands, similar customs prevailed there. About the time when he caused the idols to be destroyed, a dinner party was made, to which the principal chiefs and other persons of distinction were invited. When the company were seated around the table spread in an open bower, the king took his seat between two of his queens,—presented them with some of the forbidden food, and ate from the same dish with them. The whole company were astonished at such an innovation on ancient usages; so great, indeed, was the excitement produced, that it threatened a revolution in the government. The authority of the monarch, however, sustained by the incipient influences of Christianity, prevailed.

In 1787, the emperor of China issued the following decree. "All persons of the female sex, of whatever quality or condition, are forbidden, upon any pretext whatever, to enter a temple or quit their houses, except in cases of absolute necessity. Fathers, husbands, brothers, sons or relatives, are commanded to keep them at home, upon pain of being themselves severely punished. After this, any woman who shall enter a temple shall be apprehended and imprisoned, till some one shall appear to claim her, and to undergo the punishment due to his negligence,"—thus cutting off at a stroke the whole female population of the empire from all the rites of religion, and all the pleasures of social intercourse.

In some parts of Siberia the marriage ceremony is no sooner performed, than the wife pulls off her husband's boots, in token of submission. In other parts of the same country, the morning after a wedding, a man representing the father of the bride, delivers to the husband a whip, which, whenever the wife offends, is to be used freely. In the interior of Java the bride washes the bridegroom's feet in token of subjection. In Bambouk, Africa, she takes off her sandals, kneels before the bridegroom, pours water upon his feet, and wipes them with her mantle. In Madagascar, when a husband returns from war, his wife gives him the customary salutation of passing her tongue over his feet most respectfully. In New Holland, the slightest offence given to the husband brings down the club upon the wife, which never fails to draw forth a stream of blood and often fractures the skull. Among the Mandingoes, the terrible personage called Mumbo Jumbo, is called forth to frighten the refractory wife into submission. This demon form, assumed either by the husband himself or some one instructed by him, gives notice of his approach from the neighboring woods, near sunset, by the most frightful yells. At dark the men go out to meet him. He has a rod in his hand, a hideous mask on his head, and is fantastically decorated with the bark of trees. He is conducted to the village, where all the married women are assembled. The ceremonies commence. Songs and dances continue till a late hour. Mumbo Jumbo himself sings a song peculiar to the occasion. Then the women are required to arrange themselves in a circle. After a long pause and profound silence, Mumbo points out those that have been disobedient to their husbands, or otherwise have behaved improperly, and they are immediately seized, stripped, tied to a post, and severely beaten with Mumbo's rod, amid the shouts and deridings of the whole assembly.

And to such humiliation of woman, are boys, in some instances at least, systematically trained. The Hottentot mother, who has brought up her boy with tenderness till he has reached the period when custom demands his initiation by certain ceremonies into the society of men, is the first to feel the weight of his arm on his return home from the scene of his transition; for, to show that he is now a man and has the spirit of a man, he

A Parsee Woman of Bombay, of high rank, in full Dress.

beats her soundly; nor does censure follow the barbarous act, but he is applauded for his contempt of the society and authority of woman. For aught I know, the mother herself applauds it,—but how deep her degradation, when prepared to submit to insult like this on maternal dignity and honor! How unlike is the spirit of Christianity, prompting the son, in the perfection of his understanding, in the plenitude of his power, and amid the self-gratulations of his independence, to submit to the mild reason of his mother,—to acknowledge her unassuming sway, and admit that though independent of all things else, he cannot do without the smiles of maternal approbation, the admonitions of maternal solicitude, and the reproofs of maternal tenderness and integrity.

Woman, in unevangelized lands, is forced to perform the most perilous and menial services of the state and the family. The three thousand wives of the king of Dahomey are enrolled in the army, formed into regiments, armed with all the accoutrements of war, and a part of them serve as the king's body-guard. These numerous queens, and the other thousands belonging to the kings of Ashantee and Yarriba, are but servants, maintained for ostentation,—to display the wealth and power of their royal masters; and when not engaged in fighting the battles or guarding the persons of their lords, they are doomed to labor in the fields and submit to all the drudgery that pertains to the wife of the meanest subject of the realm. Nor is this all. At the death of an African king, his wives are slaughtered by scores and by hundreds, from an idea that their attendance will be needed in another world.

Go with me to Van Dieman's Land, and see the weaker sex charged with the whole burden of supporting their families,—husbands, children and all. Is the rough soil to be cultivated? In their hands are the implements of labor. Is the sea to be searched for the sea-carp or the lobster? They are found plunging from the projecting rocks into the briny flood, remaining on the rocky bottom, beneath the waves, twice as long (says a naval officer) as the most expert of our divers,—filling their baskets,—returning ashore,—drying themselves a few minutes by the fire, and warming their chilled limbs, and then resuming their perilous toils, while their husbands, through the whole, are seated comfortably around the fire, feasting on the choicest of the fish, and the most delicate of the broiled fern-roots.

Nor need I carry you to the other side of the globe, to witness the unseemly toils and bitter sufferings of benighted woman. Our own continent supplies us practical illustrations without end.

Let a fact or two suffice. Father Joseph (a missionary on the banks of the Oronoco) ventured to reprove an Indian female, for destroying her infant daughter. She replied, "O that my mother had thus prevented the manifold sufferings I have endured! Consider, father, our deplorable condition. Our husbands go out to hunt; we are dragged along with one infant at the breast and another in a basket. Though tired with long walking, we are not allowed to sleep when we return, but must labor the whole night in grinding maize to make chica for them They get drunk and beat us; they drag us by the hair of the head and tread us under foot. And after such a slavery of twenty years, what have we to comfort us? A young wife is brought home and permitted to abuse us and our children. What kindness can we show our daughters, equal to putting them to death? Would to God my mother had put me under ground the moment I was born!"

One case more only for the sake of contrast. "Soon after my acquaintance with these Indians," (says a missionary to the Choctaws,) "I one day saw a chief travelling on horseback, quite at his ease, followed by his poor wife, who was not only on foot, but carried his infant child, his rifle, and a quantity of provisions in a large basket at her back, supported by a strap drawn across her forehead. At a subsequent season, I met the same family again on their travels; the chief was now on foot, laden with his own arms, and he had kindly placed his wife on the saddle. The child, too, now much larger than before, was sweetly sleeping in the arms of its father, who himself seemed cheerful and happy amid the fatigues of the way." The language of the poet to his wife he practically adopted as his own:

> "On all her days let health and peace attend,
> May she ne'er want nor lose a friend;
> May some new pleasure every hour employ,
> But let her husband be her highest joy."

And what think you was the cause of this wonderful transformation? THE CHOCTAW CHIEF HAD BECOME A FOLLOWER OF CHRIST.

But the widowhood of the Pagan wife and mother is, if possible, more wretched than her married life. As if Satan could not bear that the daughters of the first victim of his seduction should find peace in any condition, he first torments them as daughters in the house of their fathers, then as wives in the dwellings of their husbands, and then as widows, cast out from

A Dancing Girl of Bengal.

every charity of human life. Under the dark covert of Pagan superstition and Mahometan delusion, unopposed by the sword of the Spirit, he accomplishes with ease his fiendish purposes, and adds the wormwood and gall of universal malice and contempt to all the bitterness of the dregs that had filled her cup of woe, from the cradle to the death of her husband. Formerly, the Caffre widow, on the decease of her husband, whatever was the season of the year, and whatever her condition, was compelled to fly to the forest, and houseless, hungry, and alone, mourn her loss day after day. During her absence her dwelling was plundered by her relatives of everything valuable, set on fire, and consumed, and the only dowry allotted her from her husband's property was a new garment, made from the hide of one of his oxen. On returning from the wildernesss, she built a new hut with her own hands, and subsisted on the avails of her own labor. Missionary enterprise has succeeded in abolishing this cruel custom, and Mr. Shaw, the missionary who was instrumental in accomplishing it, received the name of Umkinets Umfazie, (the woman's shield,) by which he is now generally known in Caffraria. In Greenland, when the husband dies, the widow, if unprotected by friends, is usually robbed of a considerable portion of her property by those who come to sympathize with her by an affected condolence, and can obtain no redress. If aged and infirm, she is not unfrequently buried alive by her own children.

As the legitimate consequences of their servile and wretched condition, females of every unevangelized land are devoid of those sentiments of delicacy, and that refined taste and acute discrimination between the lovely and the disgusting in manners and customs, which distinguish the sex in lands enlightened by the gospel. Before Christianity commenced its reign in the Society Islands, wrestling was a favorite amusement of females, and one in which those of the highest rank engaged, not only with each other, but also with the men, in the presence of thousands of spectators of both sexes. Immediately after marriage, every female provided herself with an instrument set with rows of shark's teeth, with which, on the death of any of the family, she fearfully cut and lacerated herself, beating the head, temples, cheeks, and breast, till blood flowed profusely, while she uttered the most deafening and agonizing cries. Filthy in their persons, indecent in their apparel, fantastic in their ornaments, and familiar beyond endurance in their approaches to the other sex, their character stands forth an enduring but sad monument of that intellectual and moral degradation which Paganism and Mahometanism have spread far and wide. Here their bodies are rubbed with bear's grease, and there with fish oil, or some offensive compound of vegetable and animal matter. The sheep-skin, or the bullock's hide,—the tattered handkerchief, or the entrails of slain beasts, serve for partial protection from the frosts of winter, or the burning summer's sun; and scarcely answering the purpose of fig-leaves in the fallen first pair, are not unfrequently laid aside as needless incumbrances, while the whole person is exposed to the observation of every passer-by. In Arabia, they stain their fingers and toes red; their eye-brows black, and their lips blue. In Persia, they paint a black streak around the eyes, color their eye-brows and hair, and stain the face and neck with figures of beasts, birds, flowers, &c. The Hottentot women paint the entire body in compartments of red and black. Hindu females, when they wish to appear particularly lovely, paint the body with saffron and tumeric mixed with grease. In nearly all the islands of the Pacific and Indian oceans, and in many other parts of the world, like the men, they tattoo the body, with an instrument resembling somewhat a fine-toothed comb, whose sharp teeth, dipped into a solution of indigo or soot, are thrust into the flesh, introducing the coloring matter to remain forever, and imprinting a great variety of fanciful figures on the face, the lips, the tongue, the limbs, the whole body. The process is painful, though not more so than that of the female Greenlander, who first saturates threads with soot, and then inserts them beneath the skin, and draws them through. In New Holland, the women cut themselves with shells, and by keeping open the wounds a long time, form wales or seams on the flesh, which they deem highly ornamental. And another singular addition is made to their beauty by taking off the little finger of the left hand, at the second joint,—a process performed in infancy by tying a hair around it so tight as to produce mortification. In some parts of Hindustan, at the time of marriage, a like portion of the third and little finger is removed. A similar custom prevails among the Hottentots. Among some of the savage tribes of America, and also in Sumatra and Arracan, continual pressure is applied to the skull to flatten it, and add to the beauty of its form. In nearly all the South Sea Islands, custom requires an incision to be made in the lobe of each ear, into which rolls of leaves, or long pieces of wood or ivory are inserted, and from these, shells or fish teeth are suspended, to such an amount that their weight

A KYAN WOMAN.

From a portrait taken by M. Symes, Esq., for the East India Company. Kyan is the name of a people inhabiting the mountains between Arracan and Ava. All the women of that tribe, when they arrive at a certain age, have the face tattooed. For a description of the process of tattooing, see opposite page.

draws down the ear nearly to the shoulder, and not unfrequently tears it asunder. The mother of Sumatra carefully flattens the nose of her daughter; and in New Guinea, the nose is perforated, and a large piece of wood or bone inserted, making it difficult to breathe. On the north-west coast of America, an incision more than two inches in length is made in the lower lip, and filled with a wooden plug. In Guiana, the lip is pierced with thorns, the heads being inside the mouth and the points resting on the chin. And in Java, Borneo, and Celebes, they file their teeth to a point, and color them black, considering it disgraceful to let them remain "white like the teeth of dogs."

In some countries corpulency is esteemed essential to beauty; and the wives of kings and chiefs are beloved in proportion to the sleek fatness and gross weight of their persons The Tunisian woman, of moderate pretensions to beauty, needs a slave under each arm to support her when she walks, and a perfect belle carries flesh enough to load down a camel. So anxious are mothers that their daughters should attain this unwieldy size, that they compel them to eat enormous quantities of fattening food and drink several bowls of camel's milk every day. Mungo Park describes a poor girl as crying for more than an hour, with a bowl at her lips, while her mother stood over her with a rod, and beat her cruelly, if she failed to swallow fast enough. And Capt. Clapperton found himself in not a little difficulty at Houssa, through the importunity of an Arab widow, whose wealth and rank, enforced by the charms of a huge person, black-dyed eyebrows, blue hair, red stained hands and feet, all adorned with necklaces, girdles and bracelets, seemed to fit her for the station of a queen, whither her aspirations tended, and to which, with Clapperton for a husband, she doubted not she might attain. But he happened not (O cruel!) to fancy "a walking tun-butt" for a wife, and preferred the loss of the honors of African royalty to the life-companionship of five hundred pounds of Arab flesh.

The beauty of a Chinese lady is in her feet, which in childhood are so compressed by bandages as effectually to prevent any further increase in size. The four smaller toes are turned under the foot, to the sole of which they firmly adhere. The poor girl not only endures much pain, but becomes a cripple for life. Another mark of beauty and distinction lies in the length to which the finger nails are allowed to grow,—a length that requires them to be shielded from accident by casings of bamboo. The ambitious beauties of Siam, not content with protecting carefully these ever-growing excrescences of nature, provide themselves with artificial nails four inches long.

Allow that, agreeably to the proverb, "there is no disputing of tastes," and that no nation or individual is responsible to another for peculiar customs, will it be questioned that the wearing of cumbrous and unwieldy ornaments, and the disfiguring of the body, and forcing it into uncouth forms at the expense of so much suffering, are customs offensive to nature, and to nature's God,—the legitimate progeny of Paganism?—and so far as ever grafted upon the stock of Christianity, are they more incongruous with its simplicity and at variance with its spirit, than repulsive to reason and common sense? Foolish and unseemly customs are not confined to Pagan and Mahometan females, it is true,—they exist in more enlightened lands; but in these lands, they are one after another assailed, changed and banished by the mild genius of Christianity; while, in the darker portions of the earth, they enter into the very constitution of society, and know no change or modification, more than the elements of nature, or the immemorial rites of a bloody superstition. Deplorable, then, are the delusions under which the god of this world hath bound down the nations that yield unresistingly to his sway,—severe the bondage under which they wear out hated life, and melancholy the barbarous customs, which through conscience, fancy, or caprice, his tyrant arm imposes on successive generations.

To all this may be added their unbounded superstition. Their servile fear of the gods amounts to a terror which quenches the kindlings of natural affection, and drives them on to deeds of darkest inhumanity. Ignorant of the God of love, and conceiving of their divinities as capricious, malignant and revengeful, they are easily impelled to sacrifices at which nature shudders, and every sentiment of true piety stands aghast. Unenlightened by education, and enslaved by the spirit of idolatry, they become the victims of priestly craft, without resistance, and the dupes of their own vain imaginings, as if reason and conscience entered not at all into their moral constitution. The African female ventures not to commence a journey, nor to undertake important business of any kind, till well furnished with protective charms, consisting chiefly of bits of paper, which contain a written sentence, or fragment of a sentence, carefully deposited within a bag fastened to her person. The women of Houssa, seeing Major Denham using a pen, came to him in crowds, to obtain a scrawl that should serve as an amulet to restore their beauty, to preserve the affections of their lovers, or to destroy a rival. If a child be born in Madagascar, on a day reputed unlucky, its evil destiny must be averted, by the destruction of its life, under the hands

A Hindu Woman of the Brahmin caste. She has prepared a dinner of rice, placed upon a Plantain leaf, and is carrying it to her husband.

of its parents. The only alternative is, to leave it in a narrow path, over which a herd of cattle is furiously driven, while the parents stand looking on from a distance; and if it chance to escape unhurt, they run to embrace it, convinced that the malignant influence is removed. Sometimes the child is drowned in a vessel of water prepared for the purpose, or thrown into a pit, with its face downward, or suffocated by stuffing a cloth into its mouth; but the parents themselves are commonly the executioners, under the impression that there is no other way of saving the child from the misfortunes that await its future years. From time immemorial, Hindu mothers have thrown their infant children into the Ganges, to be devoured by alligators; not because they were destitute of maternal affection, but because a mother's love was overpowered by her fears of the wrath of some offended deity. The Hindu widow burns on the funeral pile of her husband. Thus she escapes the obloquy of widowhood, and becomes entitled, as she believes, to a residence with her husband and their relatives in heaven. Thanks to the gospel of Christ, this horrid superstition has relaxed its grasp on Indian mind; but, till within a few years, thousands of widows became annually its victims; and at the death of princes and other men of elevated rank, possessed of many wives, the dreadful sacrifice has been all that Abaddon himself could desire. Twelve widows in one instance, eighteen in another, thirty-seven in another, and on the death of Ajic, prince of Malwar, fifty-eight threw themselves on the funeral piles of their husbands and perished. As late as 1844 twenty-four women were burnt in Punjab. There can be no doubt that this dreadful sacrifice is sometimes voluntary on the part of the victim, but it is by no means universally so. Not only is all the earthly glory of the deed, and the happiness of a Pagan heaven promised on the one hand, and all the terrors of contempt and persecution through life, with everlasting infamy, arrayed on the other, but force is applied, with fiend-like perseverance, to compel the unhappy wife to mount the blazing altar of Moloch.

Follow me to the immolation of a Brahmin's widow in Northern Hindustan. The unfortunate woman, of her own accord, has ascended the burning pile. The torture of the fire is more than she can endure, and by a violent struggle she throws herself beyond the reach of the flames, and tottering to a river near by, is kindly plunged into it by some English gentlemen present, to assuage her torments. She retains her senses perfectly, shrinks with dread from another encounter with the flames, and refuses so to die. Her inhuman relatives then take her by the head and feet, and throw her upon the pile, and hold her there till driven away by the heat. They endeavor too, to stun her with blows,—but again she escapes and makes to the river. Her relatives then try to drown her, but one of the English gentlemen mentioned interferes, and she throws herself into his arms, begging him to save her. "I cannot describe to you," says one present at the scene, "the horror I felt at seeing her mangled condition; almost every inch of skin on her body had been burnt off,—her legs and thighs, her arms and back, were completely raw,—her breasts dreadfully torn, and the skin dangling from them in threads,—the skin and nails of her fingers had peeled wholly off, and were hanging to the back of her hands. In fact, I never saw and never read of so entire a picture of misery as this poor woman displayed. She still dreaded being again committed to the fire, and called to us to save her. Her friends at length desisted from their efforts. We sent her to the hospital. Every medical assistance was given, but, after lingering twenty hours, in excruciating pain, her spirit departed."

Such is the superstition of heathen lands. Its forms are various, but its spirit is everywhere the same. It leads its votaries to defile themselves with the mud of the streets, to measure the distance from their homes to their temples, by the length of their bodies prostrated every six feet of the way,—to swing in the air, suspended by hooks thrust through the muscles of the back, and to submit to a thousand other tortures, in honor of some cruel but imaginary deity. It teaches the brother to betray the sister,—the mother to imbrue her hands in the blood of her own offspring,—and the son to light the pile which consumes the mother that gave him life. It glories in deeds like these, as more pleasing to the gods than any alleviation of human woe that kindness can effect, and more intrinsically meritorious than all the moral virtues commended by the philosophy of Seneca, or the precepts of Christ.

But it is time to close. We have now cursorily glanced at the character of woman, as unaffected by the refining and elevating influences of Christianity. We have seen her trodden down as the mire of the streets by him whom Heaven created to be her protector and comforter. We have seen unevangelized man everywhere, like the fabled generation of warriors springing from the serpent's teeth armed for the work of destruction, directing his chief malignities against woman,—his best friend, his safest counsellor,—his most unfailing solace,—because her native timidity and weakness invite the violence and insult of a coward-

A HINDU MOTHER LAMENTING THE DEATH OF HER CHILD.

"From time immemorial, mothers have thrown their children into the Ganges, to be devoured by alligators, not because they were destitute of maternal affection, but because a mother's love was overpowered by her fears of the wrath of some offended deity."—*P.* 161

arm! We have seen her lost to self-respect, dead to instinctive affection, ignorant of the rights with which her Maker has invested her, unacquainted with her relations to eternity, indulgent to the wildest passions of depraved nature, and plunged far down the abyss of unnatural crime. We have marked her wanderings, listened to her complaints, and seen her scalding tears. And have we no sympathy in her sufferings?—no arm that will extend to her relief?—no voice that will call her to Calvary, and direct her eye to woman's friend and Saviour, and thence to a world of unmingled purity and love? Measures are in progress (thank God!) for restoring woman to her true dignity, and re-establishing her just relations to man as her husband, guardian, and unfailing friend. The same measures will restore the world to the dominion of Christ, and man, in all his tribes, to the sway of reason and revelation. Then shall it no more be said that

> ——————" his ambition is to sink,
> To reach a depth profounder still, and still
> Profounder, in the fathomless abyss
> Of folly, plunging in pursuit of death;"

but he shall rise to "glory, honor, and immortality," and share it with the helper of his faith and love, the mother of his children, the softener of his dying pillow,—the kind angel that hovers over him as his soaring spirit takes its flight. Not far distant is the day, unless we quite mistake the "signs of the times," when, throughout all nations, woman shall resume the station Heaven first assigned her, and form again the loveliest ornament of humanity,—man's coadjutor in works of faith and labors of love, and childhood's most persuasive teacher of all that is virtuous, lovely, and of good report, in human disposition and action. Soon let that day of brightness dawn,—that glorious era be fully ushered in; for it shall prove the termination of earth's bitterest woes, and the consummation of Heaven's most earnest labors

A Thug disguised as a Merchant.

HABITS AND SUPERSTITIONS OF THE THUGS,

A SECT WHO PROFESS TO BE

DIVINELY AUTHORIZED TO PLUNDER AND MURDER.

COMPILED PRINCIPALLY FROM THE OFFICIAL DOCUMENTS OF CAPT. SLEEMAN, AGENT OF THE EAST INDIA COMPANY FOR THE SUPPRESSION OF THUGGEE

WHILE Europeans have generally travelled through India in comparative security, arising from the dread inspired by the power and dominion of the British government, the path of the native has been beset with perils by hordes of ferocious robbers, which every where abound, from the highest regions of the Himelaya Mountains to the southern extremity of Hindoostan. The most sanguinary class of these freebooters are the Thugs, or Phansigars. Their existence appears to have been entirely unknown to Europeans until about the year 1800. From January, 1826, to December, 1835, the number of Thugs committed by various magistrates amounted to 1562. Of these 328 were punished by death, 999 by transportation, 77 by imprisonment for life; from 21 security was required; 71 were sentenced to limited periods of imprisonment; making a total of 1450 convicted. Of the remainder, 21 were acquitted, 11 escaped, 31 died before sentence, and 49 were admitted evidence for the prosecution.

Gangs of Thugs sometimes consist of two or three hundred persons. In such instances, they commonly follow each other, in small parties of ten or twenty, upon roads parallel to each other, being prepared to concentrate on any point, when necessary. Different parties frequently act in concert, apprizing one another of the approach of travellers whose destruction promises a valuable booty. They assume the appearance of ordinary travellers: sometimes they pretend to be traders; and, if enriched by former spoliations, travel on horseback, with tents, and pass for wealthy merchants, or other persons of consequence. Sometimes they commence their route in more humble characters; but acquiring, in their rapacious progress, horses and bullocks, these at once furnish them with the means of transporting the remainder of their plunder, and of making pretensions to higher degrees of wealth and station.

Thugs are accustomed to wait at choultries, on the high roads, or near towns where travellers rest. They arrive at such places, and enter towns and villages, in straggling parties of three or four persons, appearing to meet by accident, and to have no previous acquaintance. On such occasions, some of the gang are employed as emissaries, to collect information, and, especially, to learn if any persons with property in their possession are about to undertake a journey. They are often accompanied by children of ten years of age and upwards; who, while they perform menial offices, are gradually initiated into the horrid practices of Thuggee, and contribute to prevent suspicion of their real character. Skilled in the arts of deception, they enter into conversation, and insinuate themselves by obsequious attentions into the confidence of travellers of all descriptions, to learn from them whence they came, whither and for what purpose they are journeying, and of what property they are possessed. When, after obtaining such information as they deem requisite, the Thugs determine to attack a traveller, they usually propose to him, under the specious plea of mutual safety, or for the sake of society, to travel together; or else they follow him at a little distance, and, when a fit opportunity offers for effecting their purpose, one of the gang suddenly throws a rope or sash round the neck of the unfortunate victim, while the rest contribute, in various ways, to aid the murderous work.

Intrepidity does not appear to be a characteristic of the Thugs; and, in truth, it is a quality not to be looked for in assassins by profession. A superiority in physical force is generally regarded as an indispensable preliminary to success. Two Thugs, at the least, are thought necessary for the murder of one man; and, more commonly, three are engaged. Some Thugs pride themselves upon being able to strangle a man single-handed; and this is esteemed a most honorable distinction. But the majority of them are, and ever have been, firm adherents of the maxim, that "discretion is the better part of valor."

Some variations have existed in the manner of perpetrating the murders; but the following seems to be the most general. While travelling along, one of the gang suddenly throws the rope or cloth round the neck of the devoted individual, and retains hold of one end, the other end being seized by an accomplice. The instrument of death, crossed behind the neck, is then drawn very tight, the two Thugs who hold it pressing the head of the victim forwards: a third villain, who is in readiness behind the traveller, seizes him by the legs, and he is thus thrown on the ground. In this situation, there is little opportunity of resistance. The operation of the noose is aided by kicks inflicted in the manner most likely to produce vital injury, and the sufferer is thus quickly despatched.

The best precautions are taken to guard against discovery or surprise. Before the perpetration of the murder, some of the gang are sent in advance, and some left in the rear of the place, to keep watch, to prevent intrusion, and to give warning, if occasion requires, to those engaged in the act. Should any persons unexpectedly pass that way before the murdered body is buried, some artifice is practised to prevent discovery, such as covering the body with a cloth, while loud lamentations are made, professedly on account of the sickness or death of one of their comrades; or one of the watchers will fall down, apparently writhing with pain, in order to excite the pity of the intruding travellers, and to detain them from the scene of murder.

Such are the perseverance and caution of the Thugs, that, in the absence of a convenient opportunity, they have been known to travel in company with persons, whom they have devoted to destruction, for several days before they executed their intention. If circumstances favor them, they generally commit the murder in a jungle, or in an unfrequented part of the country, and near a sandy place or dry watercourse. Particular tracts are chosen, in every part of India, where they may exercise their horrid profession with the greatest convenience and security. The most favorite places are much-frequented roads, passing through extensive jungles, where the ground is soft for the grave, and where the local authorities take no notice of the bodies.

In these chosen spots, a hole, three or four feet in depth, usually forms the grave of the unhappy traveller, who is placed in it with his face downwards. The barbarous character of the Thugs is displayed in their treatment of the wretched remains of the murdered persons. Though death brings a termination of suffering, it does not put an end to the outrages of the murderers. Long and deep gashes are made in various parts of the bodies: sometimes the limbs are disjointed, and the figure distorted into unusual positions. These outrages arise from various motives. Their intention generally is to expedite the decomposition of the body, and to prevent its inflation, which, by causing fissures in the superincumbent sand, might attract jackals, and thus lead to the discovery of the corpse. Sometimes, however, these deeds have been the result of disappointment, and the emanations of a petty and unmanly revenge. When the amount of plunder is less than had been expected, the villains have frequently vented their displeasure in wanton indignities on the unconscious remains of the dead.

If, when a murder is perpetrated, a convenient place for interring the body be not near, or if the Thugs be apprehensive of discovery, it is either tied in a sack, and carried to some spot where it is not likely to be found, or is put into a river or a well. In Oude, where the fields are almost all irrigated from wells, the bodies were generally thrown into them; and when the cultivators discovered these relics of crime, they hardly ever thought it worth while to ask how they came there — so accustomed were they to find them. If none of these expedients be advisable, a shallow hole is dug, in which the corpse is buried till a fit place for interring it can be discovered, when it is removed, and cut in the manner already mentioned. If compelled to perform the interment under circumstances which subject them to the risk of observation, the Thugs put up a screen on the wall for a tent, and bury the body within the enclosure; pretending, if inquiries are made, that their women are within the screen. If the traveller had a dog, it is killed, lest the affection of the animal should cause the discovery of the body of his murdered master.

Travellers resting in the same choultry with Thugs are sometimes destroyed in the night. On these occasions, a person is not always murdered when asleep; as, while he is in a recumbent posture, the stranglers find a difficulty in applying the cloth. The usual practice is, first to awaken him suddenly, with an alarm of a snake or a scorpion, and then to strangle him.

In attacking a traveller on horseback, one of the gang goes in front of the horse, and another has his station in the rear; a third, walking by the side of the traveller, keeps him engaged in conversation, till, finding that he is off his guard, he suddenly seizes the victim by the arm, and drags him to the ground, the horse at the same time being seized by the foremost villain: the miserable sufferer is then strangled in the usual manner.

Against Thugs, it must be obvious that arms, and the ordinary precautions taken against robbers, are unavailing. When a person is armed with a dagger, it is usual for one of the villains to secure his hands. It sometimes happens that entire parties of travellers, while journeying in imaginary security, are suddenly cut off. Such are the cruelty and cupidity of these wretches, that, on the presumption of every traveller possessing concealed treasure, or some property, however trifling, the greatest apparent indigence does not always afford security.

The plunder is sometimes carried home, sometimes disposed of on the road. If the murdered person resided near the place of his assassination, the property is carried to a distance: if, as is more commonly the case, he is a stranger, they do not scruple to offer the fruits of their rapine in the immediate vicinity of their crime: the only precaution taken is, that the place of sale be in advance of that where the murder was committed, and not a village where the traveller had previously been seen.

A portion of the plunder is usually appropriated to defraying the expenses of religious ceremonies; and sometimes a part is also allotted for the benefit of widows and families of deceased members of the gang. The residue of the booty, being divided into several parts, is generally shared as follows — to the leader, two shares; to the men actually concerned in perpetrating the murder, and to the person who cut the dead body, each one share and a half; and to the remainder of the gang, each one share.

The operations of the Thugs are facilitated, and their designs cloaked, by a peculiar dialect: they have recourse, also, to a variety of signs. Drawing the back of the hand along the chin, from the throat outwards, implies that caution is requisite — that some stranger is approaching. Putting the open hand over the mouth, and drawing it gently down, implies that there is no longer cause for alarm. If an advanced party of Thugs overtake any traveller whom they design to destroy, but have need of more assistance, they make certain marks on the roads, by which those of the gang who follow understand that they are required to hasten forward. A party in advance also leaves certain marks, where a road branches off, as intimations to those who are behind. They draw their feet along the dust, in the direction they have taken; and if their friends are to follow quickly, they leave the dust piled up at the end of the line where the foot drops, or make a hole in the dust with the heel. If the road afford no dust, they leave two stones, placed one upon the other, in the line they have taken, and strew a few leaves of trees along the road. If their coadjutors are to make haste, they make a very long line of leaves. They have many other signs, for similar purposes

Of the number of persons who fall victims to these lawless associations, it is obvious that no estimate can be made deserving of the slightest confidence. The number has, without doubt, varied greatly at different periods. There is reason to believe that, from the time of the conquest of Mysore, in 1799, to 1807 and 1808, the practice, in that part of India, reached its height, and that hundreds of persons were annually destroyed. In one of his reports, the magistrate of Chittoor observes, "I believe that some of the Phansigars have been concerned in above two hundred murders: nor will this estimate appear extravagant, if it be remembered that murder was their profession — frequently their only means of gaining a subsistence. Every man of fifty years of age has probably been actively engaged, during twenty-five years of his life, in murder; and, on the most moderate computation, it may be reckoned that he has made one excursion a year, and met, each time, with ten victims."

The profession of a Thug, like almost every thing in India, is hereditary, the fraternity, however, receiving occasional reënforcement from strangers; but these are admitted with great caution, and seldom after they have attained mature age.

The children of Thugs, during their more tender years, are kept in ignorance of the occupation of their fathers. After a time they are permitted to accompany them; but a veil is thrown over the darker scenes of the drama. To the novice, indeed, the expedition presents nothing but an aspect of pleasure. He is mounted on a pony; and being, by the laws of the Thugs, entitled to his share of the booty, he receives a portion of it, in presents suited to his years; the delight attending the acquisition being unalloyed by any consciousness of the means by which it has been obtained. The truth reveals itself by degrees. In a short time, the tyro becomes aware that his presents are the fruits of robbery. After a while, he has reason to suspect that robbery is aggravated by a fouler crime. At length, suspicion passes into certainty; and finally, the pupil is permitted to witness the exercise of the frightful handicraft which he is destined to pursue. The moral contamination is now complete; but it is long before the disciple is intrusted with the performance of the last atrocity. He passes through a long course of preparatory study — being first employed as a scout, next as a sexton, then as a holder of the limbs — before he is in any case thought worthy of being elevated to the dignity of a strangler.

A too precipitate disclosure of the frightful truth has some times produced fatal consequences. The following affecting story, related by a Thug who had become approver against his comrades, will illustrate this. "About twelve years ago," said the narrator, "my cousin, Aman Subahdar, took out with us my cousin Kurhora, brother of Omrow, (approver,) a lad of fourteen, for the first time. He was mounted on a pretty pony; and Hursooka, an adopted son of Aman, was appointed to take charge of the boy. We fell in with five Sieks; and when we set out before daylight in the morning, Hursooka, who had been already on three expeditions, was ordered to take the bridle, and keep the boy in the rear, out of sight and hearing. The boy became alarmed and impatient, got away from Hursooka, and galloped up at the instant the '*I hirnee*,' or signal for murder, was given. He heard the screams of the men, and saw them all strangled. He was seized with a trembling, and fell from his pony. He became immediately delirious, was dreadfully alarmed at the turbans of the murdered men, and, when any one touched or spoke to him, talked wildly about the murders, screamed as if in sleep, and trembled violently. We could not get him forward; and, after burying the bodies, Aman, myself, and a few others, sat by him while the gang went on. We were very fond of him, and tried all we could to tranquillize him, but he never recovered his senses, and before evening he died. I have seen many instances of feelings greatly shocked at the sight of the first murder, but never one so strong as this. Kurhora was a fine boy; and Hursooka took his death much to heart, and turned Byragee. He is now at some temple on the banks of the Nerbudda River."

The indiscriminate slaughter in which these miscreants might be tempted to indulge is in some degree restrained by superstition. It is deemed unlucky to kill certain castes and classes; and their members are therefore usually respected. The most important and extended exception to the general rule of murder, is that of the female sex. Thugs, who have any real regard to the principles which they profess to respect, never take the lives of women. It cannot, however, be supposed that such a rule should be invariably observed by such persons as form the society of Thugs; and, in fact, it is constantly violated. "Among us," said one of the approvers interrogated by Captain Sleeman, "it is a rule never to kill a woman; but if a rich old woman is found, the gang sometimes get a man to strangle her, by giving him an extra share of the booty, and inducing him to take the responsibility upon himself. We have sometimes killed other prohibited people, particularly those of low caste, whom we ought not even to have touched."

Among the privileged classes are washermen, poets, professors of dancing, blacksmiths, carpenters, musicians, oil-venders, sweepers, the maimed, the leprous, and those persons who carry the water of the Ganges into distant parts of India, to be used for religious purposes.

A Carrier of the Ganges Water.

The sacred cow, in the eyes of all Hindoos who have any pretensions to consistency, is a protection to its possessor; art is, however, sometimes resorted to, for the purpose of removing this impediment to business. A party of Thugs projected the murder of fourteen persons, including several women; but the design could not be carried into effect, because the victims had a cow with them. With some difficulty, they were persuaded to sell the cow to the Thugs; who, to induce the travellers to consent to the sale, pretended that they had vowed to make an offering of a cow at Shaphore, and were much in want of one. The cow was actually presented to a Brahman at Shaphore; and, the obstacle being removed, the whole of the unsuspecting travellers, including the females, were, two or three hours afterwards, strangled.

The movements of the followers of Thuggee are invariably governed by omens with which they believe their goddess favors them. However favorably an expedition may have been commenced, success is liable to be postponed by a multiplicity of ominous appearances. The dog enjoys the prerogative of putting a veto on their proceedings, by shaking his head. Sneezing entitles all the travellers within the gripe of the assassins to the privilege of an escape, and no one dares to put them to death. The fighting of cats, in the fore part of the night, is a good omen; but, if heard towards morning, it betokens evil; the evil, however, may be averted by gargling the mouth with a little sour milk, and then spirting it out. The fighting of cats during the day is a very bad omen, and threatens great evil: if the cats fall down from a height while fighting, it is still worse. These ills are beyond the healing influence of sour milk, and call for nothing less than sacrifice. The noise of jackals fighting is also a very bad omen, and involves the necessity of leaving the part of the country in which the gang hears it. Almost every sound made by animals, birds, and insects, and also their various movements, are regarded as ominous either of good or of evil. "There are always signs around us," say the Thugs, "to guide us to rich booty and to warn us of danger; and if we are only wise enough to discern them, and religious enough to attend to them, we shall prosper in all our undertakings."

The following colloquy will illustrate the opinions, entertained by Thugs generally, as to the danger of associating with those who have not been regularly educated; the importance of attending to rules and omens; and the value and excellence of Thug learning.

Capt. Sleeman. You consider that a *borka* (a leader) is capable of forming a gang, in any part of India to which he may be obliged to flee?

Sahib and *Nasir.* Certainly; in any part that we have seen of it.

Capt. S. Do you know any instance of it?

Sahib and *Nasir.* A great number. Mudee Khan was from the old Sindouse stock, and was obliged to emigrate after the attack upon that place. Many years afterwards, we met him in the Deccan; and he had then a gang of fifty Thugs, of all castes and descriptions. We asked him who they were: he told us that they were weavers, braziers, bracelet-makers, and all kinds of ragamuffins, whom he had scraped together, about his new abode on the banks of the Heran and Nerbudda Rivers, in the districts of Jebulpore and Nursingpore. He was a Mussulman; and so were Lal Khan, and Kalee Khan, who formed gangs, after the Sindouse dispersion, along the same rivers.

Capt. S. But these men have all been punished; which does not indicate the protection of Davy.

Sahib and *Nasir.* It indicates the danger of scraping together such a set of fellows for Thuggee. They killed all people indiscriminately, women and men, of all castes and professions; and knew so little about omens, that they entered upon their expeditions, and killed people, in spite of such as the most ignorant ought to have known were prohibited. They were punished, in consequence, as we all knew that they would be; and we always used to think it dangerous to be associated with them, for even a few days. Ask many of them who are now here — Kureem Khan, Sheikh Kureem, Rumzanee, and others — whether this is not true; and whether they ever let go even a sweeper, if he appeared to have a rupee about him.

Capt. S. And you think that, if they had been well instructed in the signs and rules, and attended to them, they would have thrived?

Sahib and *Nasir*. Undoubtedly! so should we all.

Capt. S. You think that an inexperienced person could not any where form a gang of Thugs of himself?

Sahib and *Nasir*. Never. He could know nothing of our rules of augury, or proceedings; and how could he possibly succeed? Does not all our success depend upon knowing and observing omens and rules?

Capt. S. It would, therefore, never be very dangerous to release such a man.

Sahib and *Nasir*. Never; unless he could join men better instructed than himself. Every one must be convinced, that it is by knowing and attending to omens and rules that Thuggee has thrived.

The practice of Thuggee is not confined to adventurers upon land. The rivers of India are infested by bands of fresh-water pirates, of similar habits to those of the land Thugs, possessing the same feeling, and differing from them only in a few trifling particulars. There is still another class of Thugs, who murder such persons only as are travelling with their children. Their only object is to secure the children and sell them into slavery.

The dark and cheerless night of superstition, which has long clouded the moral vision of India, has given rise to institutions and practices so horrible, that, without the most convincing evidence, their existence could not be credited by minds trained under happier circumstances than those which prevail in the East. That giant power, which has held the human race in chains wherever the pure and unadulterated doctrines of revelation have not penetrated, has, in India, revelled in the wantonness of prosperity; the foundations of delusion have been laid wide and deep; the poison of a false and brutalizing creed has been insinuated into every action of daily life; and the most obvious distinctions of right and wrong have been obliterated.

The fact of the existence of the cold-blooded miscreants who, in India, make a trade of assassination, is sufficiently horrible; but when it is added, that their occupation is sanctioned by the national religion, — that the Thugs regard themselves as engaged in the special service of one of the dark divinities of the Hindoo creed, — that the instruments of murder are in their eyes holy, — and that their faith in the protection of their goddess, and the perpetuity of their craft, is not to be shaken, — we must be struck by the reflection, that we have opened a page in the history of man, fearful and humiliating beyond the ordinary records of iniquity.

The genius of Paganism, which has deified every vice, and thus provided a justification of the indulgence of every evil propensity, has furnished the Thugs with a patron goddess worthy of those whom she is believed to protect. Of Kalee, the deity of destruction, they are the most devout and assiduous worshippers: in her name they practise their execrable art; and their victims are immolated in her honor. The Thugs believe that Kalee formerly coöperated more directly with them, by disposing of the bodies of those whom they murdered, but she required them not to look back to witness her operations. All was well, so long as they observed this rule; but the services of the goddess as a sextoness were lost through the carelessness or indiscreet curiosity of one of the association. Of the circumstances attendant on this mischance, there are different versions; and at least two are in pretty general circulation. According to one, a party of Thugs, having destroyed a traveller, left the body, as usual, unburied, in perfect confidence of receiving the wonted aid from the goddess. A novice, however, unguardedly looking behind him, saw the patroness of the Thugs in the act of feasting on the corpse, one half of it hanging out of her mouth. According to another report, the person looking back was a slave; and the goddess was engaged, not in satisfying the demands of hunger, or gratifying a taste for luxury by swallowing the murdered traveller, but in tossing the body into the air; for what purpose does not appear. The offence to the goddess is said, also, to have been aggravated by the fact that she was not attired with sufficient strictness to satisfy her sense of decorum. Both tales agree in representing the goddess as highly displeased, and as visiting her displeasure upon her servants, the Thugs, by condemning them to bury their victims themselves. Though she refused any longer to relieve the earth of the loathsome burdens with which her worshippers encumbered it, she was so considerate as to present her friends with one of her teeth for a pickaxe, a rib for a knife, and the hem of her lower garment for a noose. Whether or not this origin of the pickaxe be generally received, it is certain that this instrument is held by the Thugs, throughout India, in the highest veneration. Its fabrication is superintended with the greatest care; and it is consecrated to the holy duty to which it is destined with many ceremonies. In the first place, a lucky day must be fixed upon: the leader of the gang then instructs a smith to make the required tool, and the process is conducted with the most profound secrecy. The door is peremptorily closed against all intrusion; the leader never quits the forge while the manufacture is going on; and the smith must engage in no other work till his sacred task is completed. The pickaxe, being made, must next be consecrated. Certain days of the week are deemed more auspicious for this purpose than the rest: Monday, Tuesday, Wednesday, and Friday, enjoy the distinction. Care is taken that the shadow of no living thing may fall on the axe, as this would contaminate the devoted implement, and frustrate all the pains that had been taken in its formation. A doctor most deeply versed in the learning of the Thugs undertakes the solemn office of consecration. He sits down with his face to the west, and receives the pickaxe in a brass dish. The instrument which is to supply the want occasioned by the cessation of the goddess's personal labors is first washed in water, which is received into a pit dug for the purpose. The pickaxe then receives three other ablutions. The second washing is made with a mixture of sugar and water; the third with sour milk; and the fourth with ardent spirits. With red lead the pickaxe is marked, from the head to the point, with seven spots. It is again placed on the brass dish, and, with it, a cocoa-nut, some cloves white sandal-wood, sugar, and a few other articles. A fire is now kindled, and the fuel consists of dried cow-dung and the wood of the mango or byr-tree. All the articles deposited in the brass pan are, with the exception of the cocoa-nut, thrown into the fire; and when the flame rises, the Thug priest, holding the pickaxe with both hands, passes it seven times through the fire. The cocoa-nut is now stripped of its outer coat, and placed on the ground. The controller of the pickaxe, holding it by the point, then says, "Shall I strike?" The by-standers signifying their assent, he strikes the cocoa-nut with the butt-end of the pickaxe, and breaks it, exclaiming, "All hail, mighty Davy,* great Mother of us all!" The surrounding spectators respond, "All hail, Davy! and prosper the Thugs!" This is a most interesting and exciting moment; for, upon the hardness of the nut, the skill of the operator, and the accidental circumstances which may affect the force or direction of the blow, depends the realization of the hopes of the community. If the cocoa-nut be not severed at one blow, all the labor is thrown away; the goddess is understood to be unpropitious; another day must be selected for the repetition of the ceremonies, and all the trouble be incurred again. If, however, the nut is cleft at once, the proof of the approval of the goddess is indisputable. The whole of the shell, and some of the kernel of the nut, is thrown into the fire; the pickaxe is carefully tied up in a clean white cloth, and, being placed on the ground to the west, the assembled spectators, turning in that direction, prostrate themselves in adoration before "that which their own hands have made;" that which the labor of the smith might have fashioned with equal facility into an object of reverence or of contempt; and which, while it receives divine honors, is destined to assist in a series of acts most horrible and disgusting.

The ceremony of prostration concluded, all present receive a portion of the cocoa-nut. The fragments are then collected, and thrown into the pit which had been previously prepared, lest, if they remained on the ground, the sacred relics might be outraged by the defiling touch of some human foot. These ceremonies, elaborate as they are, suffice only for a single expedition.

When the sacred pickaxe is thus prepared, it must be placed in safe custody: it is not every Thug who can be trusted with it. The person who bears it is selected, principally, for his shrewdness, caution, and sobriety. It is, however, only when on a journey that it is intrusted to human care at all. When in camp, it is deposited in the earth, under the especial protection of the goddess. When buried, it is always placed with the point in the direction in which the party intend to proceed; and they have the fullest confidence that, if another course is to be preferred, the point will be found to have veered round so as to indicate the better way.

* Davy, Bhowanee, and Kalee, are different names of the same goddess.

When the pickaxe is buried, no foot must touch the earth which covers it; nor must it, at any time, be approached by an unclean animal, or any object which bears contamination. After each time that it has been used for the preparation of a grave, it must be submitted to the purification of the bath.

If the pickaxe falls from the hand of the man who bears it, dismay spreads through the gang. The omen is regarded as of the most fearful description: its horrors are aggravated by uncertainty as to the nature of the approaching evil, and even as to the party upon whom it is to descend. The omen may indicate the death of the individual who had the care of the sacred weapon, and who, through heedlessness or unavoidable fatality, suffered it to drop from his embrace; or it may forebode some dreadful reverse to the fortunes of the gang. Measures are immediately taken to frustrate the evil omen; and the first step is, to deprive the unhappy pickaxe-bearer of his office.

The enterprise in which they are engaged, whatever it be is immediately abandoned; and the pickaxe must be consecrated anew. Even these precautions are insufficient to restore things to their original state. The misfortune upon the gang is a sentence of excommunication from the society of all faithful Thugs. No other party will ever associate with one whose pickaxe has fallen, lest they should be involved in the evil which is apprehended to the "doomed ones."

The pickaxe affords the most solemn sanction of an oath among these murderers; and if any sanction can bind their consciences, it is, perhaps, the only one capable of effecting that purpose. Compared with it, neither the water of the Ganges weighs with the Hindoo, nor the Koran with the Mussulman. "If any man swears to a falsehood upon a pickaxe properly consecrated," said the Thugs, "we will consent to be hanged if he survive the time appointed. Appoint one, two, or three days, when he swears, and we pledge ourselves that he does not live a moment beyond the time. He will die a horrid death; his head will turn round, his face towards the back; and he will writhe in torture till he dies." The pickaxe is, in short, the standard around which all the gloomy family of Thug superstitions rally; it is regarded as the great source of security and prosperity. The instrument of strangulation is he d in esteem; but that of burial in infinitely more; the Thugs think of it with enthusiasm. "Do we not," said one interrogated by Captain Sleeman — "do we not worship it every seventh day? Is it not our standard? Is its sound ever heard, when digging the grave, by any but a Thug? And can any man ever swear to a falsehood upon it?" "How could we dig graves," asked another, "with any other instrument? This is the one appointed by Davy, and consecrated; and we should never have survived the attempt to use any other. No man," it was added, "but a Thug, who has been a strangler, and is remarkable for his cleanliness and decorum, is permitted to carry it."

The Thugs profess to believe that their system of murder and plunder was instituted by Kalee, the goddess whom they serve, and is, consequently, of divine origin. This they attempt to prove by the following legend: —

In remote ages, a demon infested the earth, and devoured mankind as soon as created. This devouring monster was so gigantic, that the water did not reach his waist in the unfathomable parts of the ocean; and he strode over the world unrestrained, rioting in the destruction of the human race. The world was thus kept unpeopled, until the goddess of the Thugs came to the rescue. She attacked the demon, and cut him down; but from every drop of his blood another demon arose; and though the goddess continued to cut down these rising demons with wonderful alacrity and scientific skill, other demons sprang from their blood, and the diabolical race consequently multiplied with fearful rapidity. The never-ending labor of cutting down demons, whose number was only increased by this operation, at length fatigued and disheartened the goddess. She found it indispensably necessary to make a change in her tactics; — and here the tale, which is thus far universally received, becomes subject to variations. It is admitted by all Hindoos, that the demons multiplied in the manner described; but there is a difference of opinion respecting the manner in which they were finally disposed of. The orthodox opinion is that, when the goddess found the drops of blood thus rapidly passing into demons, — a fact which, with all her divine attributes, it seems, she only learned by experience, — she hit upon a very happy expedient to prevent the blood reaching the earth, where the demoniacal transformation took place. Being furnished with a tongue of extraordinary dimensions, she, after every blow, promptly and carefully licked the blood away! A preventive check being thus placed upon the further propagation of demons, the goddess was enabled to destroy, at her leisure, those previously existing. Such is the commonly received account of the goddess's dexterity and address. That of the *Thugs* is varied, for the purpose of affording a superhuman sanction to their mode of assassination. According to Thug mythology, the goddess, when she became embarrassed by the constant reënforcements of the demon army which accrued from her labors, relinquished all personal efforts for their suppression, and formed two men from the perspiration brushed from her arms. To each of these men she gave a handkerchief; how fabricated, at a time when reels and looms were not, is a question open to the discussion of the learned. With these handkerchiefs they were commanded to put all the demons to death, without shedding a drop of blood. It does not appear why the goddess might not thus have plied the handkerchief herself: it may be presumed that she was too much exhausted by her previous exertions. Her commands, however, were faithfully executed; and the demons were all strangled without delay.

There is some difficulty in understanding how demons so powerful succumbed thus readily to two agents, who, though sprung from an exudation of the goddess's arms, were, as appears by the sequel of the tale, merely children of mortality. But the difficulty never seems to have occurred to the Thugs, whose faith, like that of the mass of their countrymen, is of a very unscrupulous character. The story is wound up with such poetical justice as might be expected in a Hindoo legend. The champions, having vanquished all the demons, offered, like honest men, to return the handkerchiefs; but their patroness, in the spirit of a grateful goddess, desired that they would retain them, not merely as memorials of their heroism, but as the implements of a lucrative trade in which their descendants were to labor and thrive. They were not only permitted, but commanded, to strangle men, as they had strangled demons. They forbore, indeed, to exercise this privilege for a long period, and several generations passed before Thuggee became practised as a profession. Whether this forbearance was founded on the principle according to which a sportsman suffers game to accumulate, is not stated. The privilege slept; but, though dormant, it was not lost; and in due time it was abundantly exercised. The lapse between the grant of the patent and the use of it might tend to raise a presumption against its having been granted; but Hindoo casuists are not accustomed to scrutinize evidence with the severity which prevails in Westminster Hall.

Interior of a Cave Temple at Ellora.

The conviction of the divine origin of Thuggee is strengthened in the minds of its followers by the belief that its mysteries are exhibited by the numerous images sculptured on the walls of the cave temples at Ellora. On this subject is the following conversation of Captain Sleeman, in the employment of the East India Company, and some Thugs who had become witnesses for the prosecution instituted against their confederates.

Capt. S. You told Mr. Johnstone, the traveller, while he was at Saugor, that the operations of your trade were to be seen in the caves of Ellora.

Feringeea. All! Every one of the operations is to be seen there. In one place, you see men strangling; in another, burying the bodies; in another, carrying them off to the graves. There is not an operation in Thuggee that is not exhibited in the caves of Ellora.

Dorgha. In those caves are to be seen the operations of every trade in the world.

Chotee. Whenever we passed near, we used to go and see these caves. Every man will there find his trade described, however secret he may think it; and they were all made in one night.

Capt. S. Does any person besides yourselves consider that any of these figures represent Thugs?

Feringeea. Nobody else. But all Thugs know that they do. We never told any body else what we thought about them. Every body there can see the secret operations of his trade; but he does not tell others of them; and no other person can understand what they mean. They are the works of God. No human hands were employed upon them; that every body admits.

Capt. S. What particular operations are there represented by the sculptures?

Sahib Khan: I have seen the sotha, (inveigler,) sitting upon the same carpet with the traveller, and in close conversation with him, just as we are, when we are worming out their secrets. In another place, the strangler has got his roomal over his neck, and is strangling him; while another, the chumochee, is holding him by the legs. These are the only two operations that I have seen represented.

Nasir. These I have also seen; and there is no mistaking them. The chumochee has close hold of the legs, and is pulling at them, *thus;* while the bhurtote is tightening the roomal round his neck, *thus!*

Capt. S. Have you seen no others?

Feringeea. I have seen these two; and also the lughas carrying away the bodies to the grave, in this manner, and the sextons digging the grave with the sacred pickaxe. All is done just as if we had ourselves done it: nothing could be more exact.

Capt. S. And who do you think could have executed this work?

Feringeea. It could not have been done by Thugs, because they would never have exposed the secret of their trade; and no other human being could have done it. It must be the work of the gods; human hands could never have performed it.

Capt. S. And, supposing so, you go and worship it?

Sahib Khan. No. We go to gratify curiosity, and not to worship. We look upon it as a mausoleum, a collection of curious figures cut by some demons, who knew the secrets of all mankind, and amused themselves here in describing them.

The high office of a strangler is not attained until after a novitiate of considerable length. When the disciple has been sufficiently prepared, or at least when he believes that the conquest of natural feeling is so far complete as to enable him to perform, without shrinking, that which he has learned to contemplate without horror, he applies to one of the most experienced and respected of the gang to become his *gooroo.* This word appears to be derived from the *goor*, or coarse sugar, which forms an important ingredient in the ceremonies of initiation; and the office of the person honored with this title is, to introduce the aspirant to the actual exercise of his profession; to instruct him in the science of hangmanship; and to preside over the rites by which the pupil is to be consecrated to his diabolical work. Precautions are taken that the young beginner may not be embarrassed by difficulties. A victim is selected, for his first essay in guilt, whose strength is below the average; and the chosen period of operation is at the moment when the senses of the traveller are bewildered by being suddenly roused from sleep. While the latter is reposing himself, the preparation takes place. The gooroo takes the pupil into a field, accompanied by three or four of the older members of the gang, and the ceremonies commence by the whole party facing in the direction in which they intend to move. The gooroo then proceeds to take the auspices; and, having invoked a favorable sign from the goddess, half an hour is allowed for the fulfilment of their wishes. If in the course of that time the required sign is obtained, all is well, and the goddess is believed to regard the attempt of the young Thug with benignity; but if no sign is obtained, or if it is of an unfavorable nature, the ambition of the novice is for that time disappointed, and the destined victim must fall by hands already practised in the murderous work.

If the sanction of the goddess be indicated, the group retire, in high spirits, to the place where the sleeping traveller awaits his death. The gooroo then, turning to the west, takes a handkerchief, and ties at one end a knot, in which he encloses a rupee. This knot is of a peculiar description, and the privilege of tying it confined to those who have been regularly introduced to their occupation. The clumsy intruder, who has not participated in the advantages derived from a regular apprenticeship to the art, leaves the end of the roomal exposed: the more accomplished practitioner manifests his science and elegance by concealing the end within the knot. This is the mark of his regular induction, and the ribbon of the order to which he has the honor to belong.

The knot being duly tied by the gooroo, the roomal is delivered to the incipient strangler, who receives it with all the reverence due to so precious a gift, bestowed by such venerated hands. The interest of the scene now increases. The executioner, attended by a *ghumgeea*, or holder of hands, stands before his victim, whose tranquil state is but an emblem of that deeper sleep which is about to seal his eyes forever. His last earthly slumber is gradually interrupted; the victim is roused for slaughter; the fatal noose is cast over his neck by the hand of the youthful assassin, and, with the aid of the attendant ruffian, the work is soon completed. One human being has passed into eternity; another has taken the last step in guilt and infamy!

The horrible work is over; and, so far from being actuated by any sensations of pity or remorse, the wretch, who has attested the strength of his nerves and the weakness of his moral perceptions, knows no feeling but that of delight, flowing from gratified ambition. To his instructor, guide, and priest, his gratitude is boundless: he bows before his gooroo, and touches his feet with both hands, in token of the deepest and most affectionate respect. But his gratitude, if confined to the person of his preceptor, would be felt to be inadequate and niggardly. The relations and friends of the reverend man are entitled to share the warm feelings of the now accomplished assassin; and to them he tenders the same homage which he has previously paid to his father in crime.

A lucky omen is once more anxiously looked for; and, as soon as it is afforded, the newly-admitted strangler opens the knot tied in the handkerchief by the hands of his tutor, and takes out the rupee which had been placed within it. This coin, with all the other silver which he has, the pupil presents to the preceptor: the latter adds his own stock of money to the offering; and, after setting apart one rupee and a quarter to the purchase of goor for the *tapoonee*, the remainder is expended in sweatmeats.

The tapoonee is a solemn sacrifice performed after every murder. The goor is placed upon a blanket or sheet, spread upon a clean spot. On the cloth, near the goor, is deposited the consecrated pickaxe, and a piece of silver for an offering. The Thug whose reputation for professional learning stands the highest, and who is supposed to enjoy the largest share of the favor of the goddess, also takes his place on the cloth, with his face to the west: the most accomplished and scientific stranglers are associated with him in this place of honor. The number of this select body must be an even one; but its extent is limited only by the size of the cloth. Those of the higher grade who are unable to find accommodation among their brethren, and the vulgar herd who have no claim to distinction, arrange themselves around the cloth which bears the sacrifice and those who preside over it. The leader then makes a hole in the ground, and, having poured into it a little of the goor, clasps his hands in the attitude of fervent devotion, and raising them, in harmony with his upturned eyes, to heaven, gives utterance to the following prayer: "Great goddess! as you vouchsafed one lac and sixty thousand rupees to Joora Naig and Koduck Bunwanee, in their need, so we pray thee fulfil our desires!" The enumeration of the precise number of thousands bestowed by the goddess upon her favorites is not very poetical; but the petition is so entirely accordant with Thug feeling, that no doubt can be entertained as to the sincerity with which it is offered. All the assembled followers repeat the prayer after the leader; and the latter, after sprinkling water on the pit and pickaxe, puts a little of the goor upon the head of each Thug who has been so fortunate as to obtain a seat upon the carpet. The signal for strangling is now given, as if a murder were actually about to be committed; and the Thugs, who have received the portions of goor, eat them in solemn silence. The most perfect stillness prevails, till these privileged persons have swallowed the precious morsels distributed to them, and diluted the repast by drinking some water. The goor is now given to all whose rank entitles them to partake of it; the greatest care being taken that no part shall fall to the ground. Should such an accident happen, the fallen fragments are carefully collected, and deposited in the pit. The misfortune is thus alleviated, so far as human prudence can avail, by preserving the hapless relics of the sugar, consecrated to murder, from contamination by the foot of man.

The sacred goor is not imparted to all Thugs indiscriminately: two conditions are necessary, to qualify them for a share of it. The participant must be in a state of freedom, servitude barring his admission to the privilege: the only remaining disqualification is found in innocence of murder. None but the practical assassin can be allowed to partake of the sacred goor; no one, but he whose hands have performed the office of strangling, is thought worthy of the food which derives its sanctity from the prayers of stranglers. For those who cannot boast the name of freemen, or whom youth, fear, or ill-fortune has withheld from performing on any of their fellow-men, the honorable act of strangulation, some sugar is set apart, before it acquires its holy character. This the excluded eat, at the time when their more favored associates partake of that portion which has been sanctified. The sweetmeats which have been provided are distributed among the gang generally.

The expedition being closed, and the members of the community having retired to their quarters, the happy individual, who has passed from a state of pupilage into the maturity of a practised assassin, entertains his gooroo at a feast as magnificent as his circumstances will afford. If he have the means of defray ing the expense, not only the immediate members of the gooroo's family, but all his relatives, are invited, and the grateful murderer equips his tutor, from head to foot, with a complete array of new vestments. The same compliment is paid to the gooroo's lady, and sometimes to all his relatives. Soon after this feast, the gooroo invites his pupil to an entertainment. The connection between them is henceforward indissoluble; and the most intimate and sacred relations of nature are considered as nothing, in comparison with it. A Thug will rather betray his father than the gooroo by whom he has been introduced to the honors of his profession.

A Thug riding in a Palanquin to a Feast prepared by his Gooroo.

The dignity and sanctity with which murder is invested by the creed of the Thugs afford lamentable proof of the inseparable connection subsisting between the corruption of religion and the corruption of morals. To obliterate all religious feeling from the heart of man is a difficult, if not an impossible task; to substitute superstitious belief for reasonable faith is, unhappily, a very easy one; and sound morals invariably disappear with sound religion. Indeed, between false religion and false morals there is a mutual action and reaction. The wayward desires of man lead him to indulge in that which true religion forbids: he therefore seeks shelter in a false one. Again; superstition sanctions, and even commands, practices against which pure morality revolts: hence the moral judgment is depraved, the restraints of conscience abolished, and that feeling which should conduct men to all that is good, and pure, and excellent, becomes the pilot to every vice, and the prompter of the most horrible crimes.

The effect of the consecrated sugar, or goor, is believed to be irresistible. Captain Sleeman, having reproached some of the fraternity on account of a murder marked by many ferocious and unmanly features, one of the party replied, "We all feel pity sometimes; but the goor of the taponee changes our nature: it would change the nature of a horse. Let any man once taste of that goor, and he will be a Thug, though he know all the trades, and have all the wealth, in the world. I never wanted food. My mother's family was opulent; her relations high in office. I have been high in office myself, and became so great a favorite, wherever I went, that I was sure of promotion; yet I was always miserable when absent from my gang, and obliged to return to Thuggee. My father made me taste of that fatal goor when I was yet a mere boy; and if I were to live a thousand years, I should never be able to follow any other trade."

A Mahometan at Prayer.

The superstitions of the Thugs are all of Hindoo origin; yet Mahometans adopt them with a belief equally implicit, and a devotion equally ardent. They pay divine honors to Kalee, the impersonation of destruction, which, in the eyes of all sound Mahometans, must be idolatry — a crime severely denounced in the Koran, and held by all good Mussulmans in abhorrence.

Their mode of escaping the difficulties in which they are involved, by the inconsistency of their creed with their practice, is illustrated by a conversation held by Captain Sleeman with some Mahometan Thugs.

Capt. S. Has Bhowanee been any where named in the Koran?

Sahib. Nowhere.

"Here," (says Captain Sleeman,) "a Mussulman Thug interposed, and said he thought Bhowanee, and Fatima, the daughter of Mahomet, were one and the same person; and that it was Fatima who invented the use of the roomal, to strangle the great demon Rukut-beejdana. This led to a discussion between him and some of my Mussulman native officers, who did not like to find the amiable Fatima made a goddess of Thuggee."

Capt. S. Then has Bhowanee any thing to do with your Paradise?

Sahib. Nothing.

Capt. S. She has no influence upon your future state?

Sahib. None.

Capt. S. Does Mahomet, your prophet, any where sanction crimes like yours; — the murder in cold blood of your fellow-creatures, for the sake of their money?

Sahib. No.

Capt. S. Does he not say that such crimes will be punished by God in the next world?

Sahib. Yes.

Capt. S. Then do you never feel any dread of punishment hereafter?

Sahib. Never. We never murder unless the omens are favorable; and we consider favorable omens as the mandates of the deity.

Capt. S. What deity?

Sahib. Bhowanee.

Capt. S. But Bhowanee, you say, has no influence upon the welfare, or otherwise, of your soul hereafter.

Sahib. None, we believe; but she influences our fates in this world; and what she orders, in this world, we believe that God will not punish in the next.

The conjoint adoration of the deities of different and discordant creeds is neither new nor uncommon in the East. In the Old Testament many instances are recorded, in which nations, as well as individuals, paid a divided homage to the true God and to a multiplicity of idols; and, in various parts of India, the Mahometans, from having long been surrounded by a Hindoo population, have been led to adopt many of their opinions and practices.

Indru, King of the minor Deities

In another interview, one of the Thug witnesses was asked—

Capt. Sleeman. And do you never feel sympathy for the persons murdered,—never pity or compunction?

Sahib. Never.

Capt. S. How can you murder old men and young children without some emotions of pity,—calmly and deliberately, as they sit with you, and converse with you, and tell you of their private affairs?

Sahib. From the time that the omens have been favorable

we consider them as victims thrown into our hands by he deity, to be killed, and that we are the mere instrument in her hands to destroy them; that if we do not kill them, she will never be again propitious to us, and we and our families will be involved in misery and want.

Capt. S. And you can sleep as soundly, by the bodies or over the graves of those you have murdered, and eat your meals with as much appetite, as ever?

Sahib. Just the same. We sleep and eat just the same, unless we are afraid of being discovered.

Capt. S. And when you see or hear a bad omen, you think it is the order of the deity not to kill the travellers you have with you, or are in pursuit of?

Sahib. Yes: it is the order not to kill them, and we dare not disobey.

Some Thugs let very poor travellers escape, in hope of finding better game: others regard forbearance, in such a case, as an act of abominable impiety. A further extract will show the respective views of these conflicting sects, and the reasoning by which they are supported.

Capt. S. When you have a poor traveller with you, or a party of travellers who appear to have little property about them, and you hear or see a very good omen, do you not let them go, in the hope that the return of the omen will guide you to better prey?

Dorgha, (Mussulman.) Let them go? Never, never!

Nasir, (Mussulman of Telingana.) How could we let them go? Is not the good omen the order from Heaven to kill them? and would it not be disobedience to let them go? If we did not kill them, should we ever get any more travellers?

Feringeea, (Brahman.) I have known the experiment tried with good effect. I have known travellers, who promised little, let go; and the virtue of the omen brought better.

Inaent, (Mussulman.) Yes; the virtue of the omen remains; and the traveller who has little should be let go; for you are sure to get a better.

Sahib Khan, (of Telingana.) Never, never! This is one of your Hindoostanee heresies. You could never let him go, without losing all the fruits of your expedition. You might get property, but it would never do you any good. No success could result from your disobedience.

Morlee, (Rajpoot.) Certainly not. The travellers who are in our hands, when we have a good omen, must never be let go, whether they promise little or much. The omen is unquestionably the order, as Nasir says.

Nasir. The idea of securing the good-will of Davy by disobeying her order is quite monstrous. We Deccan Thugs do not understand how you got hold of it. Our ancestors never were guilty of such folly.

Feringeea. You do not mean to say, that we of Murnae and Sindouse were not as well instructed as you of Telingana?

Nasir and *Sahib Khan.* We only mean to say, that you have clearly mistaken the nature of a good omen in this case. It is the order of Davy to take what she has put in our way; at least, so we in the Deccan understand it.

So long as the Thugs were faithful to their Kalee, — so long as they attended to all the rites, the ceremonies, and offerings, by which they rendered to her worship and honor, — so long as the order remained pure, and was not contaminated by the low and disreputable castes who never fail to infect those with whom they are associated, — so long they prospered in their profession, and so long did they enjoy the favor and the protection of their deity. But now, in consequence of these corruptions, they have fallen under her displeasure, and their system is likely to be exploded.

In obedience to the supposed commands of Kalee, the traveller was arrested on his journey; the ascetic was strangled on his road to Juggernaut; the young, sometimes, have had their brains dashed out against a stone, and the old have had no mercy shown to them on account of their infirmities; the beautiful female has been treated with the same ferocious cruelty as the bold and daring; the wealthy merchant has lost his life, as well as his gains and his riches; and the rajah, equipped for his journey, attended by his friends, his servants, and his train of followers, accompanied by his elephants, his horses, his camels, his oxen, and all the paraphernalia of Eastern grandeur, has, with all his attendants, been murdered in a moment. The kindness of friendship, the claims of hospitality, the interchange of social intercourse, the solemn promise, vows of protection to the young, the infirm, and the lovely, — were, by these cruel murderers, entirely disregarded; and when a kind host has been entertaining them at his table, and reposing his confidence in their brotherly regard, many of his guests have been engaged, outside the tent, in preparing his tomb, and have given him and his relatives a sepulchre, as a reward for his entertainment.

A Thug leader, possessed of most polished manners and great eloquence, being asked by a native whether he never felt compunction in murdering innocent people, answered, with a smile, "Does any man feel compunction in following his trade? and are not all our trades assigned us by Providence?" The native gentleman said, "How many people have you, in the course of your life, killed with your own hands, at a rough guess?" "I have killed none!" "Have you not been just describing to me a number of murders?" "Yes; but do you suppose I could have committed them? Is any man killed from man's killing? *Admeeke marne se koee murta.* Is it not the hand of God that kills him? and are we not mere instruments in the hand of God?"

Fatalism is a prominent dogma of the creed of the Thugs; and they consider themselves, in the exercise of their trade, to be entirely exempt from moral responsibility. Yet, in the attention to omens, or in the neglect of these instructions, they strangely enough appear to regard themselves as free agents, who may expect reward for obedience and punishment for disobedience. In their view, to commit murder is inevitable, and a matter of necessity: to murder according to rule is an act of choice; and to choose aright is meritorious.

How, it may well be asked, could such a fraternity grow up in Hindoostan, and be permitted to carry on their depredations for so many ages? But the same religion that allowed the mother to strangle her infant, that suffered the Brahmans to offer up their human sacrifices, that commanded the helpless female to mount the funeral pile, that encouraged the devotee to throw himself under the wheels of Juggernaut, patronized the Thugs in their assassinations, and gave them the license of plunder at their will. What class in the community, then, could dispute their right, or question their authority? Many of the native rajahs had licensed the infamous system; a certain tax was levied upon every house which was known to be inhabited by a Thug; and, under the sanction of the law and the government, the assassin was permitted to carry on his atrocious deeds throughout the country. Nay, such was the encouragement these murderers received, and so useful were they to the public treasury, that, when the British government resolved to put them down, and applied to the independent princes to coöperate with it in accomplishing this object, the rajah of Joudpoor contended that he had a right to protect the Thugs, and refused to give up those who had taken refuge in his territory; and had it not been for the firmness of Lord William Bentinck, who ordered an army to assemble on the frontier of his dominions, and showed him that it was impossible the Joudpoor province should become the rendezvous of a banditti who would commit their depredations with impunity upon the other states of the empire, the system would have flourished, under such protection, to this day.

Procession at a Hindu Festival.

A BRIEF DESCRIPTION

OF

TWO OF THE PRINCIPAL HINDU FESTIVALS.

In India, the division of time into weeks has all along been observed. The remembrance, however, of the *seventh* as a *Sabbath*, or *sacred day of rest*, has been completely lost. Instead thereof, there have been substituted certain periodical or anniversary days of high festival, in honor of the principal divinities. These are so numerous, that it would be impossible within our limits to describe them all, as the description would be exceedingly voluminous. Every sect has its own favorite tutelary deity, in honor of whom stated periodical festivals are held.

There is scarcely a day in the twelvemonth on which the anniversary of one or other of the gods is not celebrated by one or other of the leading sects, or sub-sects. It is quite enough for our purpose, to refer to one or two of those festivals which — from the superiority of the divinity adored, the prodigious multitudes that engage in the religious rites, and the universal suspension of business among all classes for several days — may strictly and truly be denominated *national.* In Bengal, in particular, the consort of Shiva, the destroying power, is the divinity that engrosses the largest proportion of daily, monthly, and annual devotion. Like the other principal deities, she has been manifested under an immense variety of forms. Of these a *thousand* are usually enumerated, under *as many* distinct appellations. Of the thousand forms, there are *two* that have risen to unrivalled preëminence above the rest. These are the forms of *Durga* and *Kali.* To these, therefore, our attention may be chiefly directed.*

* This description of the Durga and Kali Festivals is compiled from the writings of Rev. Alexander Duff, D. D., of Calcutta. These festivals have been witnessed by the writer and also by the compiler.

The Hindu Goddess Durga.

In the form of Durga, the consort of Shiva has been said to blend in herself the characters of the Olympian Juno and the Pallas, or armed Minerva, of the Greeks. She is, however, a far more tremendous personage than both of these combined. Having been endowed by all the gods severally with their distinctive attributes, she concentrates in herself their united power and divinity. She has thus become at once their champion and protectress. Hence her towering preëminence above them all in popular estimation; and hence, of all the annual festivals, that of Durga is most extensively celebrated in Eastern India. In this character, she is usually represented with ten arms, into which the principal gods delivered their respective weapons of warfare. From one she received the trident; from a second, a quiver and arrows; from a third, a battle-axe; from a fourth, an iron club; from a fifth, spears and thunderbolts; and so, from other gods, various other warlike instruments; together with the befitting ornaments of a golden crown, and robes magnificently adorned with jewels, and a necklace of pearls, and a wreathed circlet of snakes.

Thus martially accoutred, the belligerent goddess is ever ready to encounter the mightiest giants, and most malignant demons, that dare to invade the repose of the immortals. It was in consequence of destroying a giant, of such terrible potency as to have dispossessed the gods of their dominion, that she gained the name of Durga. As the description of this celebrated conest is a fair specimen of the manner in which the founders of Hinduism conceived and depicted those numberless battles of gods with which the sacred books abound, and as the reiterated rehearsal of it enters largely into all the meditations and prayers, the invocations and praise, the songs and the hymns, of millions of adoring worshippers, on days of high festival, it may be well to introduce the original account of it, though in a somewhat abridged form, from the volumes of Ward.

In remote ages, a giant named Durga, having performed religious austerities of transcendent merit, in honor of Brahma, obtained his blessing, and became a great oppressor. He conquered the three worlds; dethroned all the gods, except the sacred Triad; banished them from their respective heavens to live in forests; and compelled them, at his nod, to come and bow down and worship before him, and celebrate his praise He abolished all religious ceremonies. The Brahmans, through fear of him, forsook the reading of the Vedas. The rivers changed their courses. Fire lost its energy. The terrified stars retired from his sight. He assumed the forms of the clouds, and gave rain whenever he pleased; the earth, through fear, gave an abundant increase; and the trees yielded flowers and fruits out of season. The gods at length applied to Shiva. One said, He has dethroned me; another, He has taken my kingdom; and thus all the gods related their misfortunes. Shiva, pitying their case, desired his wife, Parvati, to go and destroy the giant. She willingly accepted the commission. Durga prepared to meet her with an army of thirty thousand giants, who were such monsters in size, that they covered the surface of the earth, — ten millions of swift-footed horses, — a hundred millions of chariots, — a hundred and twenty thousand millions of elephants, — and soldiers beyond the power of arithmetic to number. Parvati, having assumed a thousand arms, sat down upon a mountain, coolly awaiting the approach of her formidable foes. The troops of the giant poured their arrows at her, thick as the drops of rain in a storm; they even tore up the trees and the mountains, and hurled them at the goddess: she turned them all away, and caused millions of strange beings to issue from her body, which devoured all her enemies except their great leader. He then hurled a flaming dart at the goddess; she easily turned it aside. He discharged another; this she resisted by a hundred arrows. He levelled at her a club and pike; these, too, she repelled. He broke off the peak of a mountain, and threw it at her; she cut it into seven pieces by her spear. He now assumed the shape of an elephant as large as a mountain, and approached the goddess; but she tied his legs, and with her nails, which were like cimeters, tore him to pieces. He then arose in the form of a buffalo, and with his horns cast stones and mountains at the goddess, tearing up the trees by the breath of his nostrils; she pierced him with a trident, when he reeled to and fro. Renouncing the form of a buffalo, he reassumed his original body as a giant, with a thousand arms, and weapons in each; she seized him by his thousand arms and carried him into the air, from whence she threw him down with a dreadful force. Perceiving, however, that this had no effect, she pierced him in the breast with an arrow; when the blood issued in streams from his mouth, and he expired. The gods, filled with joy, immediately reascended their thrones, and were reinstated in their former splendor. The Brahmans recommenced the study of the Vedas. Sacrifices were again regularly performed. Every thing reassumed its pristine state. The heavens rang with the praises of Parvati; and the gods, in return for so signal a deliverance, immortalized the victory by transferring to the heroine the name of Durga.

Suppose, then, you were in Calcutta in the month of September, you might every where witness the most splendid and extensive preparations for the annual festival of Durga. In going along the streets of the native city, your eye might be chiefly arrested by the profusion of images unceremoniously exposed to sale like the commonest commodity. On inquiry, you are told that wealthy natives have images of the goddess in their houses, made of gold, silver, brass, copper, crystal, stone, or mixed metal, which are *daily worshipped*. These are stable and permanent heir-looms in a family; and are transmitted from sire to son, like any other of the goods and chattels that become hereditary property. But, besides these, you are next informed that, for the ceremonial purpose of a great festival, multitudes of *temporary* images are prepared. The reason why we call these temporary will appear by and by. These may be made of a composition of hay, sticks, clay, wood, or other cheap and light materials. They may be made of any size, from a few inches to ten, twelve, or twenty feet in height. But the ordinary size is that of the human stature. The only limitation is that of the form. This is prescribed by divine authority; and from it there must be no departure. Hence all are framed or fashioned after the same divine model. This, we may remark in passing, is one of the principal reasons why, in India, the arts of painting and statuary have for ages been stationary. These images may be made by the worshipping parties themselves, and made so small, and of substances so little expensive, that the poorest may be provided with one as well as the richest. But if the parties do not choose to make the images themselves, they can be at no loss. There is an abundance of image-makers by profession. And, alas! in a city like Calcutta, the craft of image-making is by far the most lucrative and unfluctuating of all crafts. If there be thousands and tens of thousands of families that are to engage in the celebration of the festival, there must be thousands and tens of thousands of images prepared for it.

This explains to you the origin of the spectacle presented to your eyes in passing along the streets of Calcutta. Before, behind, on the right and on the left, here, and there, and every where, you seem encompassed with a forest of images of different sizes, and piles of limbs, and bodies, and fragments of images, of divers materials, finished and unfinished, — in all the intermediate stages of progressive fabrication. But not only is the sense of vision affected; the ears, too, are assailed by the noise of implements busily wielded by the workmen. You step aside, and, standing at the door of an image-maker's workshop, you gaze with wonder at the novel process.

After the abatement of the first surprise, you are impelled to address the men. "What!" you exclaim, "do you really believe that, with your own hands, you can, out of wood, and straw, and clay, fabricate a god before which you may fall down and worship?" "No," will be the prompt reply; "we believe no such thing." "What, then, do you believe?" "We believe," respond they, "that we mould and fashion only the representative image, or graven likeness, of the deity." "How, then, come you to worship it?" "Wait," may be the reply, "till the first great day of the feast, and you will then see how it is rendered worthy of homage and adoration."

As the great day approaches, symptoms of increasing preparation thicken and multiply all around. People are seen in every direction peaceably conveying the images to their houses. The materials for wonder-stirring exhibitions and ceremonial observances are every where accumulating. Thousands of residents from a distance are seen returning to their homes in the interior, laden with the earnings and the profits of months to lavish on the great occasion. At length the government offices are by proclamation shut for a *whole week!* Secular business of every description, public or private, is suspended by land and by water, in town and in country. All things seem to announce the approach of a grand holiday — a season of universal joy and festivity.

It extends altogether over a period of fifteen days. The greater part of that time is occupied with the performance of preliminary ceremonies, previous to the three great days of worship. Early on the morning of the first of the three great days commences the grand rite of consecrating the images. Hitherto these have been regarded merely as combinations of lifeless, senseless matter. Now, however, by the power of the Brahmans, — those vicegerents of deity on earth, — they are to be endowed with life and intelligence. A wealthy family can always secure the services of one or more Brahmans; and of the very poor, a few may always unite, and secure the good offices of one of the sacred fraternity. At length the solemn hour arrives. The officiating Brahman, provided with the leaves of a sacred tree, and other holy accoutrements, approaches the image. With the two forefingers of his right hand he touches the breast, the two cheeks, the eyes, and the forehead of the image, at each successive touch giving audible utterance to the prayer, — "Let the spirit of Durga descend, and take possession of this image!" And thus, by the performance of various ceremonies, and the enunciation of various mystical verses or incantations, called *muntras*, the ghostly officiator is devoutly believed to possess the divine power of bringing down the goddess to take bodily possession of the image. The image is henceforward regarded as the peculiar local habitation of the divinity, and is believed to be really and truly animated by her. In this way, the relation of the visible image to the invisible deity is held to be precisely the same as the relation of the human body to the soul, or subtile spirit, that actuates it. The constant and universal belief is, that when the Brahman repeats the muntras, the deities must come, obedient to his call, agreeably to the favorite Sanskrit *sloka*, or verse — "The universe is under the power of the deities; the deities are under the power of the muntras; the muntras are under the power of the Brahmans; consequently, the Brahmans are gods." This is the creed of the more enlightened; but a vast proportion of the more ignorant and unreflecting believe something far more gross. It is their firm persuasion that, by means of the ceremonies and incantations, the mass of rude matter has been actually changed or transformed, or, if you will, *transubstantiated*, into the very substance of deity itself. According to either view of the subject, whether more or less rational, the image is believed to be truly animated by divinity, — to be a real, proper, and legitimate object of worship. Having eyes, it can now behold the various acts of homage rendered by adoring votaries; having ears, it can be charmed by the symphonies of music and of song; having nostrils, it can be regaled with the sweet-smelling savor of incense and perfume; having a mouth, it can be luxuriated with the grateful delicacies of the rich banquet that is spread out before it.

Immediately after the consecration of the images, the worship commences, and is continued with numberless rites nearly the whole day. But what description can convey an idea of the multifarious complexity of Indian worship? — worship, too, simultaneously conducted in thousands of separate houses; for on such occasions every house is converted into a temple. To bring the subject within some reasonable compass, you must suppose yourself in the house of a wealthy native. Let it be one which is constructed, as usual, of a quadrangular form, — with a vacant area in the centre, open or roofless towards the canopy of heaven. On one side is a spacious hall, opening along the ground floor, by many folding doors, to piazzas or verandas on either side. These are crowded by the more common sort of visitors. Round the greater part of the interior is a range of galleries, with retiring chambers. Part of these is devoted to the reception of visitors of the higher ranks, whether European or native, and part is closed for the accommodation of the females of the family, who, without being seen themselves, may, through the venetians, view both visitors and worshippers, as well as the varied festivities. The walls, the columns, and fronts of the verandas and galleries, are all fantastically decorated with a profusion of tinsel ornaments of colored silk and paper, and glittering shapes and forms of gold and silver tissue. To crown all, there is, in the genuine Oriental style, an extravagant display of *lustres*, — suspended from the ceiling, and projecting from the walls, — which, when kindled at night, radiate a flood of light enough to dazzle and confound ordinary vision.

At the upper extremity of the hall is the ten-armed image of the goddess, raised several feet on an ornamented pedestal. On either side of her are usually placed images of her two sons;—Ganesha, the god of wisdom, with his elephant head; and Kartikeya, the god of war, riding on a peacock. These are worshipped on this occasion, together with a multitude of demi-goddesses, the companions of Durga in her wars.

In the evening, about eight o'clock, the principal *pujah*, or worship, is renewed with augmented zeal. But what constitutes *pujah*, or *worship*, in that land? Watch the devotee, and you will soon discover. He enters the hall; he approaches the image, and prostrates himself before it. After the usual ablutions, and other preparatory rites, he next twists himself into a variety of grotesque postures; sometimes sitting on the floor, sometimes standing; sometimes looking in one direction, and sometimes in another. Then follows the ordinary routine of observances, [by the officiating Brahman;] sprinklings of the idol with holy water; rinsings of its mouth; washings of its feet; wipings of it with a dry cloth; throwings of flowers and green leaves over it; adornings of it with gaudy ornaments; exhalings of perfume; alternate tinklings and plasterings of the sacred bell with the ashes of sandal wood; mutterings of invocation for temporal blessings; and a winding up of the whole with the lowliest act of prostration, in which the worshipper stretches himself at full length, disposing his body in such a manner as at once to touch the ground with the eight principal parts of his body, viz., the feet, the thighs, the hands, the breast, the mouth, the nose, the eyes, and the forehead!

Then succeeds a round of carousals and festivity. The spectators are entertained with fruits and sweetmeats. Guests of distinction have *atar*, or the essence of roses, and rich conserves, abundantly administered. Musicians, with various hand and wind instruments, are introduced into the hall. Numbers of abandoned females, gayly attired, and glittering with jewels, are hired for the occasion to exhibit their wanton dances, and rehearse their indecent songs in praise of the idol, amid the plaudits of surrounding worshippers.

Another essential part of the worship consists in the presentation of different kinds of offerings to the idol. These offerings, after being presented with due form and ceremony, are eventually distributed among the attendant priests. No share of them is expected to be returned to the worshipper; so that, on his part, it is a real sacrifice. Whatever articles are once offered,

A Hindu Family carrying Offerings to an Idol.

become consecrated, and are supposed to have some new and valuable qualities thereby imparted to them. Hence the more ignorant natives often come craving for a small portion of the sacred food, to be carried home, to cure diseases.

But it is to the almost incredible profusion of the offerings presented at such festivals that we would desire to call your special attention. In general it may be said that the bulk of the people, rich and poor, expend by far the larger moiety of their earnings or income on offerings to idols, and the countless rites and exhibitions connected with idol worship. At the celebration of one festival, a wealthy native has been known to offer after this manner—eighty thousand pounds' weight of sweetmeats; eighty thousand pounds' weight of sugar; a thousand suits of cloth garments; a thousand suits of silk; a thousand offerings of rice, plantains, and other fruits. On another occasion, a wealthy native has been known to have expended upwards of *thirty thousand pounds sterling* on the offerings, the observances, and the exhibition, of a single festival; and upwards of *ten thousand pounds annually*, ever afterwards to the termination of his life. Indeed, such is the blindfold zeal of these benighted people, that instances are not unfrequent of natives of rank and wealth reducing themselves and families to poverty by their lavish expenditure in the service of the gods, and in upholding the pomp and dignity of their worship. In the city of Calcutta alone, at the lowest and most moderate estimate, it has been calculated that *half a million*, at least, is *annually* expended on the celebration of the *Durga Pujah* festival. How vast, how inconceivably vast, then, must be the aggregate expended by rich and poor on *all* the daily, weekly, monthly, and annual rites, ceremonies, and festivals, held in honor of a countless pantheon of divinities!

Ah! it is when gazing at these heaps of offering, so lavishly poured into the treasury of the false gods of heathenism, that one is constrained to reflect, in bitterness of spirit, on the miserable contrast presented by the scanty, stinted, and shrivelled offerings of the professed worshippers of the true God in a Christian land! Would that, in this respect, the disciples of Christ could be induced to learn a lesson from the blinded votaries of Hinduism! Take the case of a renowned city, the third, in point of wealth and commercial importance, in the British empire; a city on whose escutcheon and banner is inscribed the noble motto, that it is to "flourish by the righteousness of the

Word." What has been, on the part of its citizens, the manifestation of a liberality that must needs astound all Christendom, and, if it were possible, cause the very universe to resound with the never-dying echoes of its fame? Why, this great city, whose merchants are princes and the honorable of the earth, — this mighty city, that sits as a queen among the principalities of the nations, — this celebrated city did, on a late occasion, in very truth, contribute the sum of *twenty thousand pounds* tc promote, *within itself*, the cause of that Redeemer to whose vicarious sacrifice and mediatorial government it owes existence, and riches, and salvation, — all the possessions and comforts of time, — all the prospects and crowns of immortality! Well, be it so! We at once cheerfully concede that, *compared with the doings of others in this professedly Christian land*, this is one of the best and noblest specimens of modern benevolence. *But turn now to benighted Hindustan.* Look to one of its chief commercial emporia. *There*, on a *single* festival, in honor of a monstrous image of wood or clay, you find upwards of *five hundred thousand pounds* expended — not *once*, but *annually!* After this, talk, if ye will, of your liberalities. Boast of them. Eulogize them to the skies. Parade them, as munificent, in public journals. Extol them beyond measure at your great anniversaries. Would that, when next disposed to trumpet forth the praise of your own doings, ye would go and proclaim your magnificent contributions to the cause of *your* God and Savior in the presence of the deluded heathen, who replenish with free-will offerings the halls of *their* idol Durga. Ah! methinks that, instead of deigning to reply, they might point, in scornful silence, to the multiplied tokens and pledges of their own prodigal bounty, and leave you to draw an inference which might well cover you with confusion and dismay! For what could the inference be, were the silence and symbolic movement rightly interpreted and imbodied in words? What could it be but this? — "If the amount of free-will offerings be a measure of sincerity in our religious profession, surely our sincerity must be a hundred fold deeper than yours. If extent of sacrifice of worldly substance, to which we all so naturally cling, be a measure of our love to the object of worship, surely our love to our god, which you reckon a poor dumb idol, must be a hundred fold more intense than yours towards Him whom you profess to regard as the only true God and Savior. If visible fruits be the test of reality of faith, surely our faith in the truth of our religion must be a hundred fold stronger than your faith in the truth of yours. Indeed, you seem to have scarcely any faith at all. And the little you do has the appearance of being designed to save you from the charge of open infidelity, rather than to indicate a heartfelt interest in promoting the cause and honor of your God." If a rebuke so cutting, from a quarter so unexpected, do not lead to amendment and increase in your Christian liberalities, rest assured that these poor blinded idolaters, whom you affect to view with pity and compassion, will one day rise up in judgment and condemn you.

The subject of offerings is not yet exhausted. At the annual festival of Durga, there are also *bloody sacrifices* presented. The *number* of these, though in general little thought of or little known, is very remarkable. When infidel scoffers have read in the Bible of the multitude of sacrifices constantly offered, — more especially when they read of King Solomon, on one memorable occasion, sacrificing twenty-two thousand oxen and a hundred and twenty thousand sheep, — they have not scrupled to denounce the narrative as wholly beyond the pale of historic credibility — as partaking so much of the fabulous and the marvellous as seriously to damage the authenticity of the entire record that contains it. Ignorant men! ignorant of the manners and customs of Oriental nations, and, ever true to the character of your race, presumptuous in proportion to your ignorance! Were ye transported to the shores of Hindustan now, ye would find, up to this day, multitudes of sacrifices constantly offered at temples and in private houses; in single cases almost rivalling, and, collectively and nationally, vastly out-rivalling in number the thousands and tens of thousands once offered by the Hebrew monarch, at a time when the sovereign reckoned it no impiety to allocate the resources of a state to the rearing of altars and temples to Jehovah, Lord of hosts; nor, as the most exalted member of the visible church, felt it any dishonor for a season to drop the functions of royalty, and, assuming part of the office of high priest, solemnly engage in conducting the devotional exercises of a national worship. And if the overwhelming evidence addressed to your understandings had failed to convince you of the veracity of the inspired penmen, must not the testimony of sense, as to the vast numbers of Hindu sacrifices, extort from you a confession in favor of the antecedent credibility of the Jewish record in the narration of numbers not more than parallel in magnitude?

At a single temple in the neighborhood of Calcutta, the *ordinary* number of *daily* sacrifices averages between fifty and a hundred he-goats and rams, besides a proportion of buffaloes. On Saturdays and Mondays, which happen to be days particularly sacred to the divinity worshipped there, the number of sacrifices is *doubled* or *trebled;* while, on great festival occasions, the number is increased from *hundreds* to *thousands.* At the annual festival of Durga, there are hundreds of families, in the Calcutta district alone, that sacrifice severally scores of animals; many present their hecatombs; and some occasionally their thousands. It is within the present half century that the rajah of Nudiya, in the north of Bengal, offered a large number of sheep, and goats, and buffaloes, on the first day of the feast, and vowed to double the offering on each succeeding day, so that the number sacrificed in all amounted, in the aggregate, to *upwards* of *sixty-five thousand!* Mr. Ward states, that the rajah "loaded boats with the bodies, and sent them to the neighboring Brahmans, but they could not devour or dispose of them fast enough, and great numbers were thrown away."

Returning to the scene in the house of a wealthy native on the first great day of the festival:—After the worship, and the offerings, and the dancings in honor of the goddess, have been concluded, the votaries proceed, after midnight, to the presentation of animals in sacrifice. It is in the central roofless court or area of the house that the process of slaughter is usually carried on. *There* a strong upright post is fastened in the ground, excavated at the top somewhat like a double-pronged fork. In this excavation the neck of the victim is inserted, and made fast by a transverse pin above. Close at hand stands the hired executioner, usually a blacksmith, with his broad, heavy axe. And woe be to him if he fail in severing the head at one stroke! Such failure would betide ruin and disgrace to himself, and entail the most frightful disaster on his employer and family!

Each animal is duly consecrated by the officiating Brahman, who marks its horns and forehead with red lead,—sprinkles it, for the sake of purifying, with Ganges water,—adorns its neck with a necklace of leaves, and its brow with a garland of flowers,—and reads various incantations in its ears, adding, "O Durga, I sacrifice this animal to thee, that I may dwell in thy heaven

Returning from a sacrifice of animals at a Temple

for so many years." With similar ceremonies, each sacrificial victim, whether goat, sheep, or buffalo, is dedicated and slain, amid the din and hubbub of human voices. The heads and part of the blood are then carried in succession to the hall within, and ranged before the image, each head being there surmounted with a lighted lamp. Over them the officiating Brahman repeats certain prayers, utters appropriate incantations, and formally presents them as an acceptable feast to the goddess. Other meat-offerings and drink-offerings are also presented, with a repetition of the proper formulas. And, last of all, on a small, square altar, made of clean, dry sand, burnt-offerings of flowers, or grass, or leaves, or rice, or clarified butter, are deposited — with prayers, that all remaining sins may be destroyed by the sacrificial fire. This naturally leads us to answer a question that is often asked, namely, What becomes of the flesh meat of so many animals? Part of it is offered on the altar as a burnt-sacrifice. But the larger part of it always, and not unfrequently the whole, is devoured as food. The Brahmans of course have their choice; and the remainder is distributed in large quantities among the inferior castes. As it has been consecrated by being offered to the goddess, it is lawful for all who choose to partake of it.

It is impossible to note all the *variations* in the different *modes* in which the Durga Pujah is celebrated by the different castes and sects. Some individuals expend the largest proportion in peace-offerings, and meat and drink-offerings; others in bloody sacrifices and burnt-offerings: some in the dances, and the tinsel garnishings, and fire-work exhibitions; and others in entertaining and giving presents to Brahmans. The disciples of the numerous sect of Vishnu, though they celebrate the festival with great pomp, present no bloody offerings to Durga; instead of slaughtering animals, pumpkins, or some other substitute, are split in two and presented to the goddess.

The multitudinous rites and ceremonies of the first day and night of the festival being now nearly concluded, numbers of old and young, rich and poor, male and female, rush into the open area that is streaming with the blood of animals slain in sacrifice. They seize a portion of the gory dust and mud, and with the sacred compost literally bedaub their bodies, dancing and prancing all the while with almost savage ferocity. With their bodies thus bespattered, and their minds excited into frenzy, multitudes now pour into the streets — some with blazing torches, others with musical instruments; and all twisting their frames into the most wanton attitudes, and vociferating the most indecent songs, rush to and fro, reeling, shouting, and raving, more wildly than the troops of "iron-speared" and "ivy-leaved" Amazons, that were wont, in times of old, to cause the woods and the mountains of Greece to resound with the frantic orgies of Bacchus.

For two days and two nights more, there is a renewal of the same round of worship, and rites, and ceremonies, and dances, and sacrifices, and Bacchanalian fury.

As the morning of the first day was devoted to the consecration of the images, so the morning of the fourth is occupied with the grand ceremony of unconsecrating them. He, who had the divine power of bringing down the goddess to inhabit each tabernacle of wood or clay, has also the power of dispossessing it of her animating presence. Accordingly, the officiating Brahman, surrounded by the members of the family, engages, amid various rites, and sprinklings, and incantations, to send the divinity back to her native heaven; concluding with a farewell address, in which he tells the goddess that he expects her to accept of all his services, and to return again to renew her favors on the following year. All now unite in muttering a sorrowful adieu to the divinity, and many seem affected even to the shedding of tears.

Soon afterwards a crowd assembles, exhibiting habiliments bespotted with divers hues and colors. The image is carried forth to the street. It is planted on a portable stage, or platform, and then raised on men's shoulders. As the *temporary* local abode of the departed goddess, it is still treated with profound honor and respect. As the procession advances along the street, accompanied with music and songs, amid clouds of heated dust, you see human beings — yes, full-grown beings, wearing all the outward prerogatives of the human form — marching on either side, and waving their chouries, or long, hairy brushes, to wipe away the dust, and ward off the mosquitoes or flies, that might otherwise desecrate or annoy the senseless image. But whither does the procession tend? To the banks of the Ganges — most sacred of streams. For what purpose? Follow it, and you will see. As you approach the river, you every where behold numbers of similar processions, from town and country, before and behind, on the right and on the left. You cast your eyes along the banks. As far as vision can reach,

A Palankeen Bearer of the Rowaney caste dancing about the streets in celebration of the Durga Festival. *See page 217.*

they seem literally covered. It is one *living*, *moving* mass — dense, vast, interminable. The immediate margin being too confined for the contact of such a teeming throng, hundreds and thousands of boats, of every size and every form, are put in requisition. A processional party steps on board, and each vessel is speedily launched on the broad expanse of the waters. The bosom of the stream seems, for miles, to be converted into the crowd, and the movement, and the harlequin exhibitions, of an immense floating fair. When the last rites and ceremonies are terminated, all the companies of image-carriers suddenly fall upon their images. They break them to pieces, and violently dash the shivered fragments into the depths of the passing stream. But who can depict the wondrous spectacle? — the numbers without number; the fantastic equipages of every rank and grade; the variegated costumes of every caste and sect; the strangely indecorous bodily gestures of deluded worshippers; the wild and frenzied mental excitement of myriads of spectators intoxicated with the scene; the breaking, crashing, and sinking, of hundreds of dispossessed images, along the margin and over the surface of the mighty stream, — amid the loud, shrill dissonance of a thousand untuneful instruments, commingled with the still more stunning peals of ten thousand thousand human voices! Here, language entirely fails. Imagination itself must sink down with wings collapsed, utterly baffled in the effort to conceive the individualities and the groupings of an assemblage composed of such varied magnitudes.

Towards evening the multitudes return to their homes. Return, you will ask, for the purpose of refreshment and repose? No; but to engage in fresh scenes of boisterous mirth and sensual revelry. But when these are at length brought to a close, is there not a season of respite? No: all hearts, all thoughts, are instantaneously turned towards the next incoming festival, in honor of some other divinity; and the necessary preparations are at once set on foot to provide for its due celebration. And thus it has been for ages past; and thus it may be for ages to come; — unless the Christian people of these lands awake from the sleep of an ungodly, carnal security; arise from the deep slumber of sottish, selfish, luxurious enjoyment; and come forward, far beyond the standard of any present example, to advance the Redeemer's cause. O ye who do well to dwell at ease in your ceiled houses, when every where the temple of the Lord lies waste! — ye who do well to eat, and drink, and be merry, when the multitudes of the nations are up in arms against your Sovereign Lord and Redeemer, — up in arms against the true peace and everlasting happiness of their own souls, — those precious souls that will never die! — ye *may* wholly resist every appeal that is thus addressed to you at a distance, in words; but, frozen-hearted as many of you are, *could* ye, we would ask, *wholly* resist the thrilling appeal which the direct exhibition of the terrible reality would address to you?

When we have stood on the banks of the Ganges, surrounded by deluded multitudes engaged in ablutions, in order to cancel the guilt and wipe away the stains of transgressions; here assailed by the groans of the sick and the dying, stretched on the wet banks beneath "a hot and copper sky," and there stunned by loud vociferations, in the name of worship, addressed to innumerable gods; on the one hand, the flames of many a funeral pile blazing in view, and, on the other, the loathsome spectacle of human carcasses floating, unheeded and unknown amid the dash of the oar and the merry songs of the boatmen; and when we felt our own solitude in the midst of the teeming throng, — a cold sensation of horror has crept through the soul, and the heart has well nigh sunk and failed, through the overbearing impressions of sense, and the desponding weakness of faith. "Gracious God," have we exclaimed, "how marvellous is the extent of thy long-suffering and forbearance! What earthly monarch could, for a single hour, endure the thousand thousandth part of the indignities that are here *daily* offered to thy throne and majesty, O thou King of kings! And yet, thus it has been for ages! Lord, how long will it continue to be? Forever? No; no!" When we look at the apparently unchanged past, and survey the apparently unchangeable present, the review and contemplation seem to sound the death-knell of hope, that would cradle us in black despair. But when we glance at the future, as portrayed in the "sure word of prophecy," we there learn to realize the mystery of "hoping against hope." From these polluted waters of a turbid earthly stream, we turn the eye of faith to the waters of gospel grace, which are seen, in the prophetic vision, to issue from under the threshold of the temple of Zion *eastward.* They swell and deepen into a river. It is the river of life. Wherever it rolls, disease, barrenness, and death disappear.

Consigning an Image of Kali to the Ganges.

NEXT to the annual festival of Durga, one of the most popular in Eas ern India is that of the *Charak Pujah.*

Strictly and properly, this festival is held in honor of Shiva, in his character of *Maha Kala;* or *Time,* the great destroyer of all things. In this character, his personified energy, or consort, is Parvati, under the distinction and appropriate form of Maha Kali. In the annual festival held in honor of the former, the worship of the latter appears at all times to have been blended; and, in the lapse of ages, the female form of *Kali* has become a far more important and formidable personage, in the eyes of the multitude, than the male form of Maha Kala, and often engrosses more than a proportionate share of the homage and adoration of deluded worshippers. To save, therefore, the tediousness of circumlocution, and the intricacy of a perpetual double reference, we must confine ourselves to a brief notice of the goddess *Kali,* as connected with the celebration of the Charak Pujah.

It is proper, however, to state, that Brahmans, Kshattryas, and the Vaishyas, take no *active* part in the *actual* celebration of the rites peculiar to this festival. Most of them, however, contribute largely towards the expense of it, and countenance the whole of the proceedings as applauding spectators; though some of them, *in words*, profess to disapprove of many of the practices.

Of all the Hindu divinities, this goddess is the most cruel and revengeful. Such, according to some of the sacred legends, is her thirst for blood, that,—being unable, in one of her forms, on a particular occasion, to procure any of the giants for her prey,—in order to quench her savage appetite, she "actully cut her own throat, that the blood issuing thence might spout into her mouth." Of the goddess,—represented in the monstrous attitude of supporting her own half-severed head in the left hand, with streams of blood gushing from the throat into the mouth,—images may this day be seen in some districts of Bengal. The supreme delight of this divinity, therefore, consists in cruelty and torture; her ambrosia is the flesh of living votaries and sacrificed victims; and her sweetest nectar, the copious effusion of their blood.

The Kalika Purana, one of the divine writings, is chiefly devoted to a recital of the different modes of worshipping and appeasing this ferocious divinity. If, for example, a devotee should scorch some member of his body by the application of a burning lamp, the act would prove most acceptable to the goddess. If he should draw some blood from himself, and present it, the libation would be still more delectable. If he should cut off a portion of his own flesh, and present it as a burnt sacrifice, the offering would be most grateful of all. If the devotee should present *whole* burnt-offerings upon the altar, saying,—"Hrang, hring, Kali, Kali!—O! horrid-toothed goddess, eat, eat; destroy all the malignant; cut with this axe; bind, bind; seize, seize; drink this blood; spheng, spheng; secure, secure!—Salutation to Kali!."—these will prove acceptable in proportion to the supposed importance of the animated beings sacrificed. By the blood drawn from fishes and tortoises the goddess is pleased one month; a crocodile's blood will please her three; that of certain wild animals, nine; that of a bull or a guana, a year; an antelope's or wild boar's, twelve years, a buffalo's, rhinoceros's, or tiger's, a hundred; a lion's, a reindeer's, *or a man's*, (mark the combination,) a thousand; but by the blood of *three men* slain in sacrifice, she is pleased a *hundred thousand years!* Amid all the voluminous codes of Hinduism, there is not a section more loathsomely minute, more hideously revolting, than the sanguinary chapter devoted to the description of the rites and formularies to be observed at the sacrifice of *human* victims.

Under the native dynasties, it cannot be doubted that human sacrifices were very largely offered. And, even now, when this species of sacrifice has been condemned, and declared to be punishable as murder, by the British government, clearly authenticated cases do still occasionally occur. During our own brief sojourn in Calcutta, a human victim was sacrificed at a temple of Kali in its immediate neighborhood. The sacrificer was seized by the officers of justice, and capitally punished. About the same time, the governor-general felt himself called upon to strip a rajah, in the east of Bengal, of his independent rights, because, in direct violation of existing treaties, he had carried off *three* British subjects to be offered in sacrifice to Kali!

Indeed, this divinity is the avowed patroness of almost all the most atrocious outrages against the peace of society. Is there in India, as in other lands, a set of lawless men who, despising the fruits of honest industry, earn their livelihood by the plunder of their neighbors' property? At the hour of midnight, the gang of desperadoes will resort to some spot where is reared an image of Kali. There they engage in religious ceremonies, and there they offer bloody sacrifices to propitiate the favor and secure the protection of the goddess. Worshipping the instrument that is to cut through the wall of the house intended to be attacked, they address it in a *prescribed* form of words, saying,—"O instrument, formed by the goddess! Kali commands thee to cut a passage into the house; to cut through stones, bones, bricks, wood, the earth, and mountains; and cause the dust thereof to be carried away by the wind!" In full assurance of the divine blessing, and with unwavering faith in the divine protection, they hasten to the execution of their nefarious designs. How must the very foundations of even ordinary moral duties be swept away in a land where theft and plunder can be systematically carried on under the special patronage of the gods!

Again, is there in India,—as there is not, we believe, in any other land on the surface of the globe,—a still more lawless race of men,—a close, compact, confederate fraternity,—whose irresistible fate and hereditary profession it is to subsist by *murder?* These, too, well known under the name of *Thugs,* find a ready and potent protectress in Kali. To the divinely-revealed will and command of this goddess, they universally ascribe their origin, their institutions, their social laws, and their ritual observances. Intense devotion to Kali is the mysterious link that unites them in a bond of brotherhood that is indissoluble; and with a secrecy which, for generations, has eluded the efforts of successive governments to detect them. It is under her special auspices that all their sanguinary depredations have been planned, prosecuted, and carried into execution. It is the thorough incorporation of a feeling of assurance in her aid, with the entire framework of their mental and moral being, that has imparted to their union all its strength and all its terror. In their sense of the term, they are of all men the most superstitiously exact, the most devoutly religious, in the performance of divine worship. In honor of their guardian deity, there is a temple dedicated at Bindachul, near Mirzapur, to the north of Bengal. *There*, religious ceremonies are constantly performed, and thousands of animals offered in sacrifice. When a band of these leagued murderers, whose individuality and union have for ages been preserved in integrity, resolve to issue forth on their worse than marauding expedition, deliberately intent on imbruing their hands in the blood of their fellows, they first betake themselves to the temple of the goddess; present their prayers, and supplications, and offerings there; and vow, in the event of success, to consecrate to her service a large proportion of the booty. Should they not succeed, — should they even be seized, convicted, and condemned to die, — their confidence in Kali does not waver; their faith does not stagger. They exonerate the goddess from all blame. They ascribe the cause of failure wholly to themselves. They assume all the guilt of having *neglected* some of the *divinely* prescribed forms. And they laugh to scorn the idea that any evil could possibly have befallen them, had they been faithful in the observance of all the divinely-appointed rules of their sanguinary craft. How must the chief corner-stone of ordinary morality be shaken, in a land where religion is so versatile as to throw the ample shield of divine encouragement and reward over the most murderous banditti that ever appeared in human form!

If such be the general character of this goddess, what are you to expect of a festival held in honor of her lord, in his character as the *great destroyer*, — a festival in which she, too, is adored, as his destructive energy!

Most of the sectaries that embrace the form of Maha Kala as their guardian deity — belonging chiefly to the class of Shudras — are busied for several days before the festival with various initiatory ceremonies of purification, abstinence, and exercises of devotion; and those who wish to earn great merit on the occasion are engaged in preparatory operations for a whole month.

The festival itself derives its name of *Charak Pujah* from *chakra*, a discus or wheel, in allusion to the *circle* performed in the rite of *swinging*, which constitutes so very prominent a part of the anniversary observances. An upright pole, twenty or thirty feet in height, is planted in the ground. Across the top of it, moving freely on a pin or pivot, is placed horizontally an ·ther long pole. From one end of this transverse beam is a rope suspended, with two hooks affixed to it. To the other extremity is fastened another rope, which hangs loosely towards the ground. The devotee comes forward, and prostrates himself in the dust. The hooks are then run through the fleshy parts of his back, near the shoulders. A party, holding the rope at the other side, immediately begin to run round with considerable velocity. By this means the wretched dupe of superstition is hoisted aloft into the air, and violently whirled round and round. The torture he may continue to endure for a longer or shorter period, according to his own free-will; only, this being reckoned one of the holiest of acts, the longer he can endure the torture the greater the pleasure conveyed to the deity whom he serves; the greater the portion of merit accruing to himself; and, consequently, the brighter the prospect of future reward. The time usually occupied averages from ten minutes to half an hour; and as soon as one has ended, another candidate is ready, — aspiring to earn the like merit and distinction. And thus, on one tree, from five to ten or fifteen may be swung in the course of a day. Of these swinging-posts there are hundreds and thousands simultaneously in operation in the province of Bengal. They are always erected in the most conspicuous parts of the towns and villages, and are surrounded by vast crowds of noisy spectators. On the very streets of the native city of Calcutta, many of these horrid swings are annually to be seen, and scores around the suburbs. It not unfrequently happens that, from the extreme rapidity of the motion, the ligaments of the back give way, in which case the poor devotee is tossed to a distance, and dashed to pieces. A loud wail of commiseration, you now suppose, will be raised in behalf of the unhappy man who has thus fallen a martyr to his religious enthusiasm. No such thing! Idolatry is cruel as the grave Instead of sympathy or compassion, a feeling of detestation and abhorrence is excited towards him. By the principles of their faith, he is adjudged to have been a desperate criminal *in a former state of being;* and he has now met with this violent death, in the present birth, as a righteous retribution, on account of egregious sins committed in a former!

The evening of the same day is devoted to another practice almost equally cruel. It consists in the devotees' throwing themselves down, from a high wall, the second story of a house, or a temporary scaffolding often twenty or thirty feet in height, upon iron spikes or knives that are thickly stuck in a large bag or mattress of straw. But these sharp instruments being fixed rather loosely, and in a position sloping forward, the greater part of the thousands that fall upon them dexterously contrive to escape without serious damage. Many, however, are often cruelly mangled and lacerated; and, in the case of some, the issue proves speedily fatal.

At night, numbers of the devotees sit down in the open air, and pierce the skin of their foreheads; and in it, as a socket, place a small rod of iron, to which is suspended a lamp that is kept burning till the dawn of day, while the lamp-bearers rehearse the praises of their favorite deity.

Again, before the temple, bundles of thorns and other firewood are accumulated, among which the devotees roll themselves uncovered. The materials are next raised into a pile, and set on fire. Then the devotees briskly dance over the blazing embers, and fling them into the air with their naked hands, or toss them at one another.

Some have their breasts, arms, and other parts, stuck entirely full of pins, about the "thickness of small nails, or packing-needles." Others betake themselves to a vertical wheel, twenty or thirty feet in diameter, and raised considerably above the ground. They bind themselves to the outer rim, in a sitting posture, so that, when the wheel rolls round, their heads point alternately to the zenith and the nadir.

But it were endless to pursue the diversity of these self-inflicted cruelties into all their details. There is one, however, of so very singular a character, that it must not be left unnoticed. If the problem were proposed to any member of our own community to contrive some other distinct species of torture,—amid the boundless variety which the most fertile imagination might figure to itself, probably the one now to be described would not be found. Some of these deluded votaries enter into a vow. With one hand they cover their under-lips with a layer of wet earth or mud; on this, with the other hand, they deposit some small grains, usually of mustard-seed. They then stretch themselves flat on their backs, — exposed to the dripping dews of night and the blazing sun by day. And their vow is, that from that fixed position they will not stir, — will neither move, nor turn, nor eat, nor drink, — till the seeds planted on the lips begin to sprout or germinate. This vegetable process usually takes place on the third or fourth day; after which, being released from the vow, they arise, as they dotingly imagine and believe, laden with a vast accession of holiness and supererogatory merit.

To the south of Calcutta is a spacious, level plain, between two and three miles in length, and a mile, or a mile and a half, in breadth. On the west it is washed by the sacred Ganges, on whose margin, about the middle of the plain, Fort William rears its ramparts and battlements. Along the north is a magnificent range of buildings, — the Supreme Court, the Town Hall, with other public edifices, — and, in the centre, most conspicuous of all, the arcades, and columns, and lofty dome of Government House. Along the whole of the eastern side, at short intervals, is a succession of palace-like mansions, occupied as the abodes of the more opulent of the European residents. In front of this range, facing the west, and between it, therefore, and the plain, is the broadest and most airy street in Calcutta, well known under the name of Chowringhee. Chiefly to the north of the plain, and partly to the east, beyond the ranges of European offices and residences, lies the native city, — stretching its intricate mass of narrow lanes, and red brick houses, and "hive-like" bamboo huts, over an extent of many miles, and teeming with *half a million* of human beings! At a short distance from the south-east corner of the plain, across a narrow belt of low suburban cottages, lies the celebrated temple of Kali-Ghat. The grand direct thoroughfare towards it, from the native city, is along the Chowringhee road.

Thither, early, before sunrise, on the morning of the great day of the Charak festival, we once hastened to witness the extraordinary spectacle.

From all the lanes and alleys leading from the native city, multitudes were pouring into the Chowringhee road, which seemed at every point to symbolize the meeting of the waters, — realizing, through its entire length, the image of a mighty confluence of innumerable living streams. The mere spectators could easily be distinguished from the special devotees. The former were seen standing, or walking along with eager gaze; arrayed in their gayest holiday dress, exhibiting every combination and variety of the snow-white garb and tinsel glitter of Oriental costume. The latter came marching forward in small isolated groups, — each group averaging, in number, from half-a-dozen to twelve or fifteen, and constituted somewhat after this manner: Most of the party have their loose robes and foreheads plentifully besprinkled with vermilion or rose-pink. Two or three of them are decked in speckled or party-colored garments, uttering ludicrous, unmeaning sounds, and playing off all sorts of antic gestures, not unlike the merry-andrews on the stage of a country fair. Two or three, with garlands of flowers hanging about their neck, or tied round the head, have their sides transpierced with iron rods, which project in front, and meet at an angular point, to which is affixed a small vessel in the form of a shovel. Two or three, covered with ashes, carry in their hands iron spits or rods of different lengths, small bamboo canes or hookah tubes, hard-twisted cords, or living snakes whose fangs had been extracted, — bending their limbs into unsightly attitudes, and chanting legendary songs. Two or three more are the bearers of musical instruments — horned trumpets, gongs, tinkling cymbals, and large, hoarse drums surmounted with towering bunches of black and white ostrich feathers, which keep waving and nodding not unlike the heaving, sombre plumes of a hearse; and all of them belabored as furiously as if the impression were, that the louder the noise, and the more discordant the notes, the better and more charming the music. Thus variously constituted, the groups of devotees were proceeding along. On looking behind, one group was seen following after another as far as the eye could reach; on looking before, one group was seen preceding another, as far as the eye could reach; — like wave after wave, in interminable succession.

Besides these groups of worshippers, who are reckoned pre-eminent in holiness and merit, there are others that advance in processions, bearing various pageants, flags, banners, models of temples, images of gods, and other mythological figures, with portable stages on which men and women are engaged in ridiculous and often worse than ridiculous pantomimic performances

Hundreds of these processions spread over the southern side of the plain, presenting a spectacle so vast and varied — so singular and picturesque — that the pencil of the most skilful artist would not be dishonored if it failed in adequately representing it.

At the extremity of Chowringhee, the road towards the temple narrows considerably. The throng is now so dense that one is literally carried along. On approaching the precincts of the sacred shrine, it is found surrounded by a court and high wall. After entering the principal gate, which is on the western side, the temple itself starts up full in view. To the south of it is a spacious open hall or portico, elevated several feet above the ground, and surrounded by a flight of steps, above which rise a range of pillars that support the roof. Between the portico and the temple is a narrow pathway, along which the stream of spectators was flowing; while the groups of the devotees marched round the side farthest from the temple. Being of the number of the spectators, we mingled with the teeming throng that pressed on, with maddening frenzy, to obtain a glimpse of the idol. Here one and another would start aside, and knock their heads against the temple wall or brick pavement, muttering incantations to command the attention and attract the favor of the goddess. It may here be noticed, in passing, that a temple in India is not, like a Christian church, a place for the disciples to assemble in and engage in reasonable worship; but it is ordinarily designed as merely a receptacle for the senseless block of the idol, and a company of Brahmans, as its guardian attendants. Hence, as there is not much occasion for light, there are few or no windows. The light of day is usually admitted only by the front door, when thrown wide open. Darkness is thus commingled with light in the idol cell, and tends to add to the mysteriousness of the scene. The multitudes all congregate without; but there is no *preaching* in their "halls of convocation;" no devotional exercises to raise the soul on the wings of heavenly contemplation; no instructions in the knowledge of the true God or the plan of a complete salvation; no inculcation of motives to lead to the forsaking of sin; no animated exhortations to the cultivation of virtue and piety: all, all, is one unchanging round of sacrifice and ceremony — of cruelty, and sport, and lifeless form.

Standing immediately opposite the temple gate, we saw on either side stationed, as usual, a party of Brahmans, to receive the proffered gifts. On one side lay a heap of flowers, that had been consecrated by being carried within and presented to the goddess; on the other side, a large heap of money, — copper, and silver, and gold, — that had been contributed as free-will offerings. To the spectators, as they passed along, the Brahmans were presenting consecrated flowers, which were eagerly carried off as precious relics; and, in exchange for them, the joyous votaries threw down what money they possessed. And this they did as profusely as it was assuredly done cheerfully and without a grudge. Ah, here again were we painfully reminded of the state of things, as regards *liberality on principle*, in Christian lands. What a contrast to our meagre and half-extorted contributions, in the cause of Christian benevolence, was presented by the spectacle at the temple of Kali-Ghat! "What!" was one led to exclaim, — "what! is it really so, that error is fraught with a mightier charm than truth? — that a foul and sanguinary superstition can operate on the soul more effectually than the benign religion of heaven? — that ignorance is more powerful than divine knowledge? — that heathenish custom is superior in efficacy to enlightened principle? — and that the fear of a dumb idol can exert a more potent influence than the love of a bleeding, dying Savior? Ah, if this be so, what can our inference be, except that, amongst us, almost every one ought to bear about him a frontlet between his eyes, inscribed with the motto, 'Profession, not principle!' — and that almost all, having a name to live, are nevertheless dead in spiritual lethargy and slumber, and deaf to the most sacred claims of duty towards God and man!"

And one's wonder could not be diminished, when he looked within the temple, and, in the midst of the "darkness visible," beheld the horrid block of the idol that had succeeded in conquering men's selfishness, and in turning the stagnant pool of grasping covetousness into a running stream of lavish liberality. The figure within this temple is, in several of its parts, for what reason we know not, somewhat incomplete; but it is still sufficiently frightful and hideous. In the sacred legends the goddess is constantly described, and, in the thousands of images that are annually made of her, she is almost uniformly delineated, as a female of black or dark-blue complexion, dancing savagely on the body of her own husband. She is represented with four arms, having in one an exterminating sword, and in another a human head held fast by the hair; a third points downwards, "indicating the destruction that surrounds her," and the fourth is raised upwards, "in allusion to the future regeneration of nature by a new creation." She is represented with wild, dishevelled hair, reaching to her feet. Her countenance is most ferocious. Her tongue protrudes from a distorted mouth, and hangs over the chin. She has three eyes, red and fiery, one of which glares in her forehead. Her lips and eyebrows are streaked with blood, and a crimson torrent is streaming down her breast. She has ear-rings in her ears; but what are they?—they are the carcasses of some hapless victims of her fury. She has a girdle round the waist; but what is it?—it is a girdle of bloody hands, said to have been cut off the wounded bodies of her prostrate foes. She has a necklace round the neck; but what is it?—it is a necklace of ghastly skulls, said to have been cut off the thousands of giants and others slain in her battles. And such is the monster-divinity, who, on that day, calls forth the shouts, and acclamations, and free-will offerings, of myriads of adoring worshippers!

Passing now to the eastern side of the court, we soon saw what the groups of devotees were to be engaged in. Towards the wall there were stationed several blacksmiths, with sharp instruments in their hands. Those of a particular group, that carried the rods, canes, and other implements, now came forward. One would stretch out his side, and, getting it instantly pierced through, in would pass one of his rods or canes. Another would hold out his arm, and, getting it perforated, in would pass one of his iron spits or tubes. A third would protrude his tongue, and getting it, too, bored through, in would pass one of his cords or serpents. And thus, all of a group that desired it had themselves variously transpierced or perforated. When these had finished, another group was waiting in readiness to undergo the cruel operation; and so another and another, apparently without end.

Several groups, then returning, mounted the steps of the portico in front of the temple, to prepare for their most solemn act of worship. But O, how impotent must human language ever be in the attempt to convey an adequate impression of the scene that followed!

Those of the different groups, that carried in front the vessels already referred to, now ranged themselves all around the interior of the colonnade. All the rest assembled themselves within this living circle. On a sudden, at a signal given, commenced the bleating, and the lowing, and the struggling, of animals slaughtered in sacrifice at the farthest end of the portico; and speedily was the ground made to swim with sacrificial blood. At the same moment of time, the vessel-carriers threw upon the burning coals in their vessels handfuls of Indian pitch, composed of various combustible substances. Instantly ascended the smoke, and the flame, and the sulphureous smell. Those who had the musical instruments sent forth their loud, and jarring, and discordant sounds. And those who were transpierced began dancing in the most frantic manner, — pulling backwards and forwards, through their wounded members, the rods and the canes, the spits and the tubes, the cords and the writhing serpents, till their bodies seemed streaming with their own blood! All this was carried on *simultaneously*; and that, too, within a briefer period of time than has now been occupied in the feeble and inadequate attempt to describe it! Again and again would the loud shouts ascend from the thousands of applauding spectators — shouts of "Victory to Kali! Victory to the great Kali!"

O, as we gazed at the harrowing spectacle, how was the soul, by the resistless force of contrast, hurried away to more highly-favored climes! Yes; — standing though we were at the distance of fifteen thousand miles from our native land, how did the soul, with lightning speed, flee across intervening oceans and continents, and, in the chambers of imagery, revive and realize the visions of other days! When we thought of the land of our fathers, — when we contrasted the pure, peaceful, soul-elevating exercises of its Sabbaths, with the scene of infernal revelries then before our view, — how could we help exclaiming, "Surely, if the former be a fit emblem and harbinger of that eternal Sabbath which rolls over heaven's bright inhabitants, this other scene must be an emblem and harbinger of the restless tossings of the burning lake!" And O, is it possible that, if Christians were transported hither to gaze, but for a single moment, on such a master-triumph of Satanic delusion, — is it conceivable that they could give sleep to their eyes, or slumber to their eyelids, till they entered a vow in heaven to do all that in them lay to demolish such a hideous fabric of idolatry and superstition, and rear the beauteous temple of Christianity upon the ruins?

In conclusion, therefore, we would, with our whole heart, and strength, and soul, call upon all, who profess to be disciples of the Lord Jesus, to come forward now "to the help of the Lord to the help of the Lord against the mighty." We call upon you by that wondrous scheme, for the redemption of a ruined world, which from all eternity engaged the counsels of the God-head, to compassionate the poor, dying, perishing heathen; — not to allow the prince of darkness any longer to trample on his miserable victims without control, or drag them as unresisting captives along the broad road that leadeth to perdition. We call upon you by the miseries of earth, the torments of hell, the joys of heaven, — by all that the Savior has done and suffered in his vicarious obedience, and agony, and bloody sweat, — to come forth now and be instrumental in erecting the standard of the cross on the downfall of the crescent and the ruins of paganism; and thus to snatch from the regions of woe the souls of many who may be fitted to sing the praises of Jehovah and the Lamb! We call upon you, by your own eternal destiny, not to allow the fountain of divine benevolence, once opened on the hill of Calvary, to remain there from age to age shut up and sealed — a mere spectacle of solitary, and useless, and barren grandeur. But come now, and draw therefrom in copious streams; replenish your reservoirs; fertilize the soil; and thus produce a rich harvest of fruit, which, when the earth and all the works therein are burnt up, and the visible heavens are no more, will increase in beauty, and flourish forever on the shores of a blissful immortality!

A

DESCRIPTION OF THE SHASTERS.

BY J. J. WEITBRECHT,

FOR MANY YEARS A RESIDENT IN INDIA.

A LEARNED Brahmin, on being asked how many volumes their Shasters contained, replied, "Who is able to calculate that? No man can number them; the palace of the Rajah of Burdwan would not contain them; they are like the ocean, unfathomable, without measure, and without end."

That celebrated searcher into Hindu mythology, Sir William Jones, appeared to coincide in the same view, when, in astonishment and surprise, he exclaimed, "To whatever part of this literature we may direct our attention, we are every where struck with the thought of infinity." The Iliad of Homer numbers twenty-four thousand verses, but the Mahabharat of the Hindus four hundred thousand; and the Purannas, comprehending only a small portion of their religious books, extend to two millions of verses.

The Hindus divide the voluminous masses of their Shasters into eighteen parts, asserting that they contain eighteen distinct kinds of knowledge. To the first class belong the FOUR VEDAS. The Brahmins believe these to be as old as eternity. They also assert that they were communicated to mankind, not through the medium of a mortal, but by the mouth of Brahma himself.

The Vedas consist of a compilation of prayers, called *Muntrus;* and, at a later period, a collection of doctrines and precepts, which are called *Brahmanas,* was added. They detail an endless number of ceremonies which are to be performed by the priest, the ascetic, and the hermit, at their religious services.

One of the oldest sages of Hindu antiquity collected the Brahmanas, or religious statutes from the Vedas, into special tracts, with the title of *Upanishads.* This compilation is a kind of compendium of Hindu theology, generally known under the appellation of *Vedanta.*

There have been men, professed Christians, who have spoken with enthusiastic admiration of the Hindu writings. Their primitive religion, it has been said, contained the most sublime doctrines, and inculcated the most pure morality. But this is an egregious delusion. "Many an object appears beautiful when seen at a distance, and through a mist; but, when you approach it nearer, you will smile at the deception. As you become more intimately acquainted with the Shasters, you must feel struck with the absurd character of their doctrines, and the laxity of their morals."

The second class of sacred books treat on the art of healing, music, war, architecture, and sixty-four various mechanical arts. Hence you perceive the Shasters of the Hindus teach not merely religion, but every kind of science and knowledge. By far the most numerous class of Shasters is comprehended in the poetical works of the Purannas, treating on the creation of the world, the power and attributes of the gods, the incarnations of Vishnu, &c. Among the most interesting of these may be numbered the Mahabharat and Bhagavat Gita. The latter contains a description of Krishna's life. The Ramayun, an epic poem, gives a history of Ram, an incarnation of Vishnu. The historical details afford remarkable specimens of the ancient history of Hindustan. In the preface of the Ramayun it is stated, "He who constantly hears and sings this poem will obtain the highest bliss, and will become like the gods."

Besides these, there is an endless mass of writings, counted sacred, namely, the Nyay Shasters, the Smritis, the Mimangsa, of philosophical, juristical, and metaphysical tendency.

The age of the Vedas has never been ascertained with any degree of certainty. Some enthusiastic admirers of them put them far before the time of the deluge. A learned professor in America actually requested Sir W. Jones to search among the Hindus for the Adamic books. The amazing credulity of skeptics and unbelievers, in every thing except the records of the Sacred Scriptures, is notorious. The latter gentleman, who is regarded as one of the most profound scholars in Hindu antiquity, concluded, from internal and external evidence, the age of the Vedas to be about three thousand years; accordingly, they stand in antiquity nearest to the books of Moses. All the other Sanscrit writings are of more recent date.

After this cursory glance into the impenetrable chaos of Hindu Shasters, we proceed a step farther. The question we have now to consider is this: *What view has the Brahmin of a Divine Being?* and we shall be sadly mistaken if we expect to find in the Hindu Shasters a confession of faith laid down which the learned uniformly acknowledge as the groundwork of their belief.

As a north-wester hurricane in Bengal, after a glowing, fiery, hot day, mingles clouds with dust, leaves, wood, and earth, in its destructive course, so we find in the wild confusion of the Shasters all the nobler divine thoughts, and purer ideas of the majesty of God, interwoven and mixed up with the most puerile nonsense. You cannot lay your hand on one point of doctrine, which is not in conflict with another, or denied by some rival system.

The Hindu, however, acknowledges *one Supreme Being as the ground and foundation of his religion.* "Ek Brumho, dittyo nashti," — One God, and beside him no other, — this sentence is become a proverb, and is in the mouth of every Brahmin. His writings dignify this supreme and eternal Being with the title "Brahm," which is to be carefully distinguished from Brahma, an emanation of the former, and the first person in the Hindu trinity. The Shasters describe Brahm as a being without beginning and without end, almighty, omniscient, unchangeable; in short, as being possessed of all the divine attributes, as the sublimest conceptions of the Holy Scriptures describe Jehovah. This being, however, all spirit and without form, is devoid of qualities. The Shasters declare that the very idea of allowing attributes in Brahm renders a multiplication of him a necessary consequence. For this very reason, the Brahmin will not allow the God of the Bible, because to him it appears impossible and irrational to believe that spirit can act and create without being united with matter.

Brahm is therefore represented without mind, without will, without consciousness of his existence. No wonder that many Hindus, in going one step farther, declare the Supreme is nothing; for a spirit without power and energy is like a thing of nought. Nevertheless, it is asserted, on the other hand, that he enjoys the highest beatitude, — it is the bliss of a deep, uninterrupted sleep.

Brahm, however, must one day have awaked from his long sleep; or, in other words, the negative character of his existence must have changed into the positive. This was necessary for calling the world into existence. On this important point, the different philosophical systems, headed by their respective leaders, have carried on a never-ceasing warfare.

Brahm awoke, say the Vedas, and, feeling desire arising, said, "Let me be many." Forthwith he took upon himself a material form; and henceforth he is like a spider, sitting in the centre, spinning out his interminable threads, and fastening what he produces from himself to the right and, left, towards all quarters of the infinite vacuum.

Here, then, the shell of Hinduism begins to open; the creation of the world, according to *its* teaching, is nothing more or less than a manifestation of Brahm in visible material forms. It is the most perfect system of pantheism. The cosmogony of the Shasters runs thus: All the germs or seed corns of the world that was to come into existence were condensed in the shape of an egg, and the supreme took possession of it in the form of Brahma. One year of the creation, or one thousand jugs, which, according to our reckoning, makes three hundred millions of common years, elapsed before the egg was hatched. During that long period, it was swimming like a bubble upon the mighty deep or chaos; its brightness resembled that of a thousand suns. At last it broke, and Brahma sprang forth. His appearance was terrific; he had a thousand heads, a thousand eyes, and a thousand arms — a suitable complement to undertake the work of creation. Another monstrous being escaped from the egg with him, evidently signifying the crude materials from which the great mundane machine was to be prepared. The hairs of this monster were the trees and plants of the forests, his head the clouds, his beard the lightning, his breath the atmosphere, his voice the thunder, his eyes the sun and moon, his nails the rocks, his bones the mountains of the earth. When the egg was fabricated, Brahm, as creator, retired from the scene; and henceforth he troubled himself no longer with the concerns of the world. He relapsed into his former sleep, and nothing will disturb him in his dreams until the time when the dissolution of the present universe is to awaken him to renewed activity.

No temple in India is consecrated to this "unknown God." The reason of this is obvious: the Hindu expects nothing, fears nothing, hopes nothing from a god who is asleep, wrapped up in sweet dreams, and who has communicated his power to those who are now managing the government of the world as his delegates.

When the great egg opened, it brought forth, likewise, the three worlds, viz., the uppermost, which is inhabited by the gods, the middle, intended for the dwelling-place of man, and the infernal world, destined to be the habitation of demons and all sorts of fearful beings.

The earth, according to the description of the Shasters, is a flat plain of circular form, resembling the water-lily, measuring four hundred millions of miles in circumference. The inhabitable part of it consists of seven islands of similar shape, each of which is surrounded by an ocean. The innermost island, bounded by the ocean of salt water, is called *Jampadwip;* the second island is surrounded by a sea consisting of the juice of the sugar-cane; the sea surrounding the third contains spirituous liquors; the fourth, clarified butter; the fifth, sour milk; the sixth, sweet milk; and the seventh contains sweet water. Beyond the latter there is a land of pure gold, but inaccessible to man; and far beyond it extends the land of darkness and the hell. The earth is resting upon an enormous snake with a hundred heads, and the snake upon a tortoise. Whenever the former shakes one of his heads, an earthquake is caused thereby. The bigoted Brahmin is firmly persuaded of the indubitable fact, that no circumnavigator of the globe has ever succeeded in passing beyond the salt-water ocean; and let the English become ever so skilful in the art of navigation, they will always be obliged to sail within its confines.

In the centre of the vast plain of the earth, which is two hundred and fifty thousand miles in diameter, the loftiest of all mountains, Sumeru, rises to the enormous height of more than two hundred thousand miles. It is crowned with three golden summits, which are the favorite residences of Brahma, Vishnu, and Shiva. The highest clouds reach to about a third part of the height of the mountain. At the foot of this mountain there are three smaller hills, placed like sentinels, on the top of each of which grows the mangoe-tree, above two thousand miles in height. These trees bear a fruit, as delicious as nectar, which measures several hundred feet in diameter. When it falls to the ground, juice exudes from it, whose spicy fragrance perfumes the air; and those who eat thereof diffuse a most agreeable smell for many miles around them. The rose-apple-tree is likewise growing on those hills, the fruit of which is as large as an elephant, and so full of juice that at the season of maturity it flows along in a stream, and whatever it touches in its course is changed into the purest gold. Here is a specimen of geography, which surpasses all *our* preconceived and short-sighted notions of the globe we inhabit!

I mentioned above that the cosmogonies in the mythology of the Hindus are many. One of the most popular among them deserves to be noticed. The god Vishnu slept in the depth of the ocean. From him grew a water-lily, which swam on the surface of the water, and out of which proceeded Brahma, to whom the gods delivered the work of the creation of the universe. In order to accomplish his purpose, he led for a long time the life of an ascetic. But he was unsuccessful. The disappointment drove him into a rage, and the tears gushed from his eyes. Out of these briny drops arose gigantic beings of terrific shape. One of his deepest sighs over this sad catastrophe produced the god Rodru, that is, light and warmth, who, upon Brahma's request, undertook the continuation of the arduous task. But it did not proceed in his hands. Brahma was therefore obliged to resume it again; and, after much anxiety, various beings issued from his fingers, ears, and other members. The work then advanced with more success; and fire, earth, and wind, followed each other in quick succession.

Upon this, Brahma divided himself into human forms, and created men; then he assumed the shape of a bullock, and afterwards that of a horse, and thus produced the various kinds of four-footed animals, birds, &c. In this way the uncounted multitudes of animated beings, which now people the earth and other worlds, rose gradually into existence.

Thus you see how the idea of pantheism pervades the base fiction of this very absurd and immoral history of the creation. To create is, in fact, nothing but a manifestation of Brahma in new forms; he becomes an elephant, a mountain, a river; and thus he produces and propagates the different species of living beings. The whole universe is a portion of himself. In this view he is represented in the Vedas: "Brahma is not separated from the creation: he is the light of the sun, of the moon, and of the fire; the Vedas are the breath of his nostrils; the primitive elements are his eyes; the shaking movements of events are his laugh; his sleep is the destruction of the world. In various forms he enlivens the creature: in the form of fire, he digests their nourishment; in the form of air, he preserves their life; as water, he quenches their thirst; as the sun, he ripens the fruits; as the moon, he gives them refreshing sleep. The progress of time is the step of his foot. Brahma hears and sees every thing. He cultivates the field; he is turned into a cloud to give it moisture; he becomes corn and satisfies mankind. While he dwells in the body, he sustains its vital warmth; if he withdraw, it will get cold and die. He destroys sin in the devout, as the cotton thread is singed in the fire. He is the source of all truth and of all lies. He who takes his refuge to him will become holy; he who turns his face from him will become a blasphemer." Such is one of the most sublime songs which the priests sing in honor of their Creator.

The distinction of caste is traced in its origin to the *creation of man.* By successive emanations from himself, Brahma called various classes of mankind into existence. First the Brahmin escaped from his mouth, as the representative of God in human form. The nature of his birth signified him to be, not only the highest and most exalted of all human beings, but likewise the intended teacher, and the mediator between the gods and mankind. From the arm of Brahma, the defence of the body, sprung the Kshutryu, or the caste of warriors; the object of whose creation was evident, from the nature of his birth: he was to protect the people by his powerful arm, and to shield and defend his brethren against the aggression and oppression of the wicked. From Brahma's breast issued the Voishnu, or caste of merchants and tradesmen, to provide for the necessities of mankind; and from the humblest member, his foot, came the despised Sudra, or the servile caste. Their allotted task was to perform every kind of menial labor for their nobler-born brethren, both at home and in the field.

The Sudras constitute by far the greatest number of the inhabitants of Bengal; and probably it is the same in other parts of India. For thirty centuries past have those unhappy beings groaned under the curse of the haughty Brahmin, and patiently borne the intolerable burden. "What God has appointed," say they, "we cannot alter." So holy and unchangeable is this institution of castes, in the eyes of the people, and so firm is the belief of the Hindu as to the appointment being of divine authority, that a transition from one caste to the other is absolutely impossible. A prince cannot purchase the Brahminical thread, which is the badge of their dignity, for millions. As a mouse can never be changed into an elephant, or the thorn-bush into an orange-tree, so neither can a Sudra be turned into a Brahmin. The Brahmin may sink: if he offend against his caste, his holiness will withdraw itself; he forfeits his nobility and is degraded. If he marry the daughter of a Sudra, his progeny will be a sort of illegitimate caste. Accordingly, at the present day, Brahmins of the first, second, and third class, are met with in India. The purest and most honored are, of course, those who, both on the paternal and maternal side, have derived their descent from ancestors of pure blood.

In modern times, however, the castes have been considerably intermixed with each other. The Kshutryus were nearly extirpated, even before the country was conquered by the Mohammedans, because they resisted the dominion of the Brahmins. The Voishnus, or merchants' caste, is no longer found in Bengal, and it is believed that they have been amalgamated with, and lost among, the Sudras; while these latter have, especially in Southern India, sunk down almost to a level with the brute creation.

The laws of the Hindus are peculiarly calculated for the preservation of the power and authority of the priests. In the time when Hinduism was in its flower, the Brahmin could in no wise be touched. The prince dared not execute him, though he might have committed every possible crime. As flesh and blood are pervaded in him by divine holiness, his moral character must be judged by quite a different standard to that of the Sudra. A good action possesses with him a much higher value; and the most hideous crime loses in his case a great deal of its heinous nature. When a Brahmin robbed his Sudra brother, he had to pay a fine in money; but, when the latter was the offender, he had to be burned at the stake; and, if he took a Brahmin by his beard, the law commanded his hands to be cut off. Yea, the revenge of this hateful priest pursued the poor wretch into the other world; for, if a Sudra should meet him in an irreverential manner, he will after death become a tree; and, should he venture to cast an angry glance at him, Yama, the god of the lower regions, will tear out his eyes; or, if he beat the Brahmin but with a straw, he will in twenty transmigrations be born of impure beasts.

India is, like Italy, a paradise for priests. All the offerings which the Hindu presents to his gods fall, as a matter of course, to the Brahmin. He that feeds a number of them has the promise of all the blessedness of heaven. The dying Hindu, who leaves him in his will some of his goods and cattle, will, freed from sin, enter forthwith into Shiva's heaven. He who sells his cow will go to hell; but, if he make it over to a Brahmin, he will go to heaven. He who presents him an umbrella will be protected against the injurious influence of the sun; if any one will give him a pair of shoes, his feet will not be blistered on a journey; and if a person honor him with gifts of aromatic spices, he will be preserved from offensive smells and exhalations all his days.

The husbandman may not cultivate his field, — he may not put the sickle into the ripe corn, — without first giving the Brahmin his due. He is the first at court, and in attendance on the Rajah. In the most fertile parts of the country, in towns and villages, where the inhabitants are in comfortable circumstances, Brahmins are found in the greatest numbers. In the western parts of Bengal, where forests abound, and where the ground is less productive, they are but rarely seen; they "love to eat the fat, and drink the sweet," and have taken good care to obtain both for their portion.

SPECIMENS OF THE SHASTERS.

From the Shiva Puran, Part II.

SUTA'S NARRATIVE.

"Hear, O Rishi! * a most excellent and sin-destroying narrative, which I will relate as I heard it with other Rishis from Vyasa. Formerly there was a famous Rishi, named *Gautama*, and his virtuous wife was named *Ahalya;* with her he performed, during a thousand years, a rigorous *tapas* † in the southern country, near the mountain Brahmadri. At this time a drought had desolated the country, and neither moisture nor rain had the earth experienced for a hundred years; water there was not; and ascetics, men, birds, and beasts, died every where. On beholding this lamentable state, Gautama, having reflected, performed for six months the severest mortifications in honor of Varuna; at the termination of which the god appeared to him and thus said: 'I am propitiated by thee, O holy devotee! Demand whatever boon thou wishest, and I will grant it.' Gautama then requested rain; but Varuna replied, 'How can I transgress the divine command? Ask some other boon, which it may be

* Saint.

† A *tapas* is a course of severe penance, either to propitiate a divinity or for other purposes, and the advantage derived from it is always superhuman.

in my power to bestow upon thee.' On hearing this, Gautama said, 'O god! if thou art pleased with me, and willing to grant me a favor, I will request that which thou canst easily perform: cause, then, to appear a hermitage which shall surpass all others in beauty, and shaded from the sun by fragrant and fruit-bearing trees, where men and women by holy meditation shall be liberated from pain, sorrow, and anxiety; and also, as thou art the lord of water, let it enjoy a perennial fountain.' Varuna replied, 'So be it;' and then, causing a pit to be filled with water, he thus said: 'This water shall remain unexhausted, and thy name shall become celebrated by this reservoir becoming a place of pilgrimage.' Having thus spoken, Varuna disappeared. In this manner did Gautama obtain water, with which he performed in due manner the daily ceremonies. He sowed, also, rice for holy offerings, and watered it from this inexhaustible fountain; and grain of various kinds, trees, flowers, and fruits adorned his hermitage. Thus the grove of Gautama became the loveliest on the terrestrial orb; and there resorted ascetics, birds, and beasts, to live in happiness; and there, likewise, holy men fixed their abode with their sons and disciples. In this grove none knew sorrow, and gladness alone prevailed. But listen to what afterwards happened.

"On one day Gautama had sent his disciples to bring water; but, when they approached the fountain, some Brahmin women who were there prevented them, and scoffingly called out, 'We are the wives of holy anchorets; after we have filled our pitchers, you may then draw water.' The disciples returned, and mentioned this circumstance to the wife of Gautama; and Ahalya, having consoled them, proceeded herself to the fountain, and, having drawn water, brought it to her husband. Thus she did daily; and the other Brahmin women not only scoffed her, but at length went, and thus each falsely addressed her husband: 'My lord! Ahalya daily taunts me and the other Brahmin women, and I have no other resource than thee. Violence, falsehood, deceit, foolishness, covetousness, and inconsiderateness, are the innate vices of women; and, alas! of what avail will holy meditation be to me if I suffer every day the reproaches of Ahalya?' Each husband, having heard these words, revolved them in his mind, and thought that they could not be true, and that they would be guilty of ingratitude if they noticed them. But their wicked wives every day reproached them for not affording them redress; and at length, one day, as they were passing through the grove, they overheard their wives making the same complaints to Gautama, and therefore believed that what they had said was true. The devotees, having then assembled together, began to consult respecting the manner in which they might resent this injury, so that their revenge might not appear to proceed from them; and, after deliberation, determined on invoking the assistance of Ganesha. They then propitiated him with offerings of durwa, lotoses, and rice; of vermilion, sandal-wood, and incense; of rice-milk, cakes, and sweetmeats; and with prostrations, prayers, and burnt-offerings. Well pleased, the god appeared and thus spoke: 'I am propitiated: say, what boon do you desire?' They replied, 'If thou art willing to grant us a favor, contrive to remove Gautama from his hermitage; for, if we adopt any means for that purpose, we shall expose ourselves to censure.' Ganesha answered, 'To injure or destroy a man who is free from blame is not just; and to return evil for good will be productive of sorrow, and not of benefit. Whoever performs holy meditation will obtain the happiest result; but the injuring of another will destroy the advantages which would be derived from it. Gautama has given you gold, and you wish to return glass; but that which is right ought to be performed.' Having heard these words, the devotees, from mental delusion, thus replied: 'O lord! we entreat thee to do what we have requested, as we desire no other favor.' Ganesha then said, 'Good cannot produce evil, nor evil good: from its very essence, evil must produce misery, and good happiness. Gautama will enjoy happiness from his holy meditation; but sorrow alone can result from your present wish. But you are deluded by female fascination, and you cannot, therefore, discriminate between good and evil. I will, however, comply with your request; though you will undoubtedly hereafter regret having made it.' Having thus spoken, Ganesha disappeared.

"Gautama, unacquainted with the evil intentions of the devotees, joyfully performed each day the sacred ceremonies; but one day, being in a field of rice and barley, Ganapati, having assumed the form of an extremely debilitated cow, appeared there trembling, and scarcely able to move, and began to eat the rice and barley. Observing this, the compassionate Gautama lifted a stalk of grass and struck the cow with it, in order to drive her away; but scarcely was she touched with the stalk when she dropped on the ground, and immediately died, while all the devotees beheld what passed with looks of distress. The holy men and their lovely wives then exclaimed, 'O Gautama! what hast thou done?' Gautama, also, in amazement, thus addressed Ahalya: 'What an accident! How can I have incurred the anger of the gods? what shall I do? where shall I go? thus involved in the guilt of the murder of a cow!' The devotees at the same time thus reproached him: 'Alas! O holy Rishi! of what avail has been thy knowledge? Alas! of what avail thy burnt-offering and thy strict performance of every ceremony?' In the same manner, their wives thus reproached the wife of Gautama: 'Alas! Ahalya, of what avail have been thy wisdom, and the universal respect shown to thee? Alas! of what avail thy virtue and piety?' Thus they reviled Gautama and his wife, and then exclaimed to each other, 'Let us not look on the face of this slayer of a cow: whoever looks on his countenance will become equally guilty; and whoever approaches his hermitage, that man's offerings neither will fire nor the manes receive.' Thus reviling Gautama, they all threw stones at him. Gautama then exclaimed, 'Alas! alas! what shall I do? I swear, O holy men! that I will depart from this place.' Having thus spoken, he removed to a distant spot, and there erected a hermitage; but as long as this sin, falsely imputed to him, remained unexpiated, he could perform no holy ceremony, and his wife continued exposed to the insults of the other Brahmin women; and thus Gautama suffered the greatest misery. At length, after a short time, Gautama assembled the holy men, and thus addressed them: 'Have compassion on me, and acquaint me with the ceremonies by which my sin may be expiated; for without instruction no good act can be effected.' The Brahmins then consulted together respecting the penance which ought to be prescribed, while Gautama stood at a distance in an humble posture; and, after deliberation, they thus said: 'Sin can never be expiated except by suitable purification; for this purpose, therefore, do thou circumambulate the whole earth, and, on returning here, circumambulate a hundred times the mountain of Brahma, and thus thou wilt be purified; or make ablutions in the Ganges, and on its banks, having made ten millions of earthen lingams, worship the god whose symbol is the lingam, and then perambulate the sacred mountain and bathe in the hundred holy pools. By these means thy sin will be expiated.' Having heard these words, Gautama first circumambulated the holy mountain; and afterwards, as directed, formed the earthen lingams, in order that he might be restored to his pristine purity. He then, with

Ahalya, and his disciples, worshipped Shiva with the holiest rites and most intense devotion. At length the lord of the mountain-born goddess descended from the summit of Kailasa and thus addressed him: 'Say, what boon dost thou desire?' On beholding that form divine, a sight of which is so difficult to be obtained, Gautama was filled with delight, and, having reverenced the mighty god with laudatory strains, requested that he would liberate him from the guilt that he had incurred. Shiva

Gautama, or Budh.

replied, 'Happy art thou, O mighty Rishi! and the fruit of all thy pious acts hast thou obtained, for thou art free from sin. Thou hast been deceived by these wicked men, for even the three worlds become purified by thy presence. How, then, canst thou be polluted by an act committed by these evil-minded men, and who will suffer for it hereafter?' Shankara * then explained to him all their wickedness and ingratitude, and Gautama listened with astonishment; and after Shankara had ceased speaking, he thus said: 'These Brahmins have done me the greatest favor, for, if it had not been for their act, I should not have enjoyed the felicity of beholding thee, O lord!' Pleased with these words, Shiva again expressed his satisfaction with the piety and devotion of Gautama, and desired him to ask a boon. Gautama replied that all he entreated was, that the Ganga [the River Ganges] might there appear, in order that he might purify himself in it. With this request Shiva complied; and the consequence was the establishment of the sacred place of pilgrimage at Trimbucka, on the Godavery."

Gautama is the principal divinity of the Burmese. According to tradition, he was so offended with the Brahmins that he determined to separate himself from them and establish a new religion.

From the Matsya Puran.

A DELUGE.

Suta, addressing the Sages: — "Formerly, there was a king named Manu, distinguished by every virtue; who, having resigned his kingdom to his son, withdrew to a certain spot, and there, indifferent to pain and pleasure, performed the severest devotional penance for a hundred thousand years. At length Brahma appeared to him and said, 'Choose whatever boon thy mind desires.' The king, bowing to Brahma, thus replied: 'From thee one most excellent boon I crave; and wish that, when the *pralaya* takes place, I may be preserved from that destruction in which all things movable and immovable shall be involved.' 'So be it,' Brahma replied, and then disappeared; and the angels rained on the king from heaven a shower of flowers.

"Some time after, as near his hermitage he was offering water to the *manes*, a small fish came into his hands along with the water; and the compassionate king, in order to preserve it, placed it in a small vessel. But in one night it increased sixteen inches in size, and exclaimed, 'Save me! save me!' The king

* *Shankara* is another name for Shiva. Some of the Hindu divinities have many names, and they are used interchangeably, to prevent repetition.

The Chinese Budh.

Brahma

Brahma

then successively threw it in a jar, a well, a lake, and a river; but, in each night, the fish grew larger, and entreated a more roomy place of abode. At length the king threw it into the sea, when it immediately occupied with its bulk the whole ocean. Manu, then alarmed, exclaimed, 'What god art thou? or canst thou be any other than Vasudeva, whose form has thus expanded to such immensity? I know thee now; but why hast thou thus pained me, by assuming the form of a fish, O Keshava! Praise be to thee, O Vishnu, lord of the universe!' The lord replied, 'Excellent! excellent! Thou hast discovered the truth, O sinless one! Know that in a short time this earth shall be submerged in water, and that this ship has been prepared by all the gods for thy preservation. When, therefore, the deluge takes place, enter this ship, and take with thee all kinds of seeds, and of animals that are produced from heat, from eggs, or from the womb; and fasten it to this horn of mine. Thus shalt thou be preserved, and after the deluge has ceased, shalt thou become, on the renovation of the world, the progenitor of all beings; and thus shall a holy devotee, steadfast in ascetic practices, and completely conversant in divine knowledge, become, at the beginning of the Krita Yug, the lord of a manwantara.' Having thus spoken, the lord disappeared, and Manu continued his devotions to Vasudeva until the deluge took place, as foretold by Vishnu; and then Janardana appeared in the form of a horned fish; and, while the ship into which Manu had entered was attached to its horn, Vishnu, under the form of this fish, in answer to the questions of Manu, revealed unto him the Matsya Puran."

From the Bhagawat, Book III. Chap. 13.

THE EARTH RAISED FROM THE WATERS OF A DELUGE.

"Parameshti, then, beholding the earth sunk amidst the waters, long meditated on the means by which it might be replaced in its former situation. 'Whose divine aid,' he thought, 'shall I implore to upraise from the deep abyss that earth which I formerly created? That lord from whose heart I sprang can alone effect this mighty work.' As Brahma thus resolved, suddenly from his nostrils sprang a young boar, no larger than the thumb; but, as he viewed it, in an instant it wonderfully increased to the size of a mighty elephant. The Rishis Prajapatis, Rumaras, and Manu, beholding the boar-like form in astonishment, thus in their minds conjectured: 'What can be this delusive form of a boar, since, in reality, it must be of a divine nature? How wonderful that it should spring from Brahma's nostrils no larger than the top of the thumb, and, in an instant, become equal to a mighty mountain! Can it be that mighty lord, on whom we meditate with minds devout?' While thus they thought, that lord, who was the primeval victim, emitted a sound loud as thunder, and, as the eight regions reëchoed the sound, Brahma and his sons were delighted; for they hence knew the lord, and, their anxiety being dissipated, the pure inhabitants of Janalok, Tapalok, and Satyalok, united in addressing to him their holy praise. Pleased with these praises, the wondrous boar displayed himself like a vast mountain, with tail erect, mane waving, his bristles sharp as lances, and hoofs striking the sky, and snuffing, in imitation of a boar, to discover the earth. Then he of the terrible tusk, with terror-divested eyes regarding those who were adoring him, like a sportive elephant dived into the abyss of waters; and the waters being divided, as if a thunderbolt vast as a mountain had fallen precipitately into them, resounded like the thunder; and, raising in pain its wide billows, the abyss profound exclaimed, 'Save me, O lord of sacrifice!' Thus, subduing the waters with his sharp hoofs, he reached their utmost extremity, and saw lying there the earth, which he had originally intended for the abode of souls. Having then slain the demon Hiranyaksha, he uplifted it on his tusks from the dark abyss, and Brahma and his sons extolled his wondrous power."

From the Padma Puran, Chap. 5.

DAKSHA'S SACRIFICE.

Pulastya, addressing Bhishma: — "Formerly, O Bhishma! Daksha prepared a sacrifice at Gungadwara, to which came all the immortals and divine sages. At this festival celestial viands abounded. The consecrated place of sacrifice extended for several yojanas. Numerous altars were erected. The sacred rites and ceremonies were duly performed by Vasishta, Angiras, Vrihaspati, and Narada; and Vishnu protected the sacrifice. But Sati thus addressed her father: 'My lord! all the immortals, the divine sages, and my sisters with their husbands, adorned in the costliest manner, have honored this festival with their presence; and I observe that not a single one has been uninvited except my husband. But, unless he attend, empty will be all these rites, and

Vishnu.

Huneman.

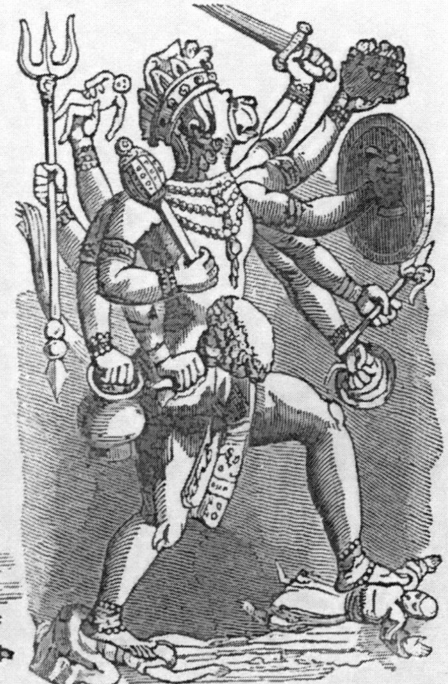

Huneman

productive of no advantage. Say, then, has it been through forgetfulness that thou didst not invite my lord?' On hearing these words, Daksha, with parental affection, placed his youthful daughter, who showed such fondness for her husband, in his lap, and thus replied: 'Listen, my darling! while I explain the reason why thy husband has not been invited. It is because that he is the bearer of a human skull, a delighter in cemeteries, accompanied by ghosts and goblins, naked or merely clothed with a tiger's or elephant's skin, covered with ashes, wearing a necklace of human skulls, ornamented with serpents, always wandering about as a mendicant, sometimes dancing and sometimes singing, and neglecting all divine ordinances. Such evil practices, my darling! render thy husband the shame of the three worlds, and unworthy to be admitted at a sacrifice where Brahma, Vishnu, and all the immortals and divine sages, are present.' He ceased, and Sati, incensed by his words, with anger-inflamed eyes thus spoke: 'That god is the lord of the universe, from whom all things and beings have received their rank and station, and whose supreme excellence no tongue is able to declare; and, though delighting in cemeteries, covered with ashes, and adorned with human bones and serpents, he is the creator, the provider, and the preserver. It was alone through the favor of Rudra [Shiva] that Indra obtained heaven; through the will, also, of Rudra, Brahma creates; and, were it not for Rudra, how could Vishnu have the power to preserve? If, therefore, I have derived might from my devotion, and if I be beloved by Rudra, since thou hast despised him, this sacrifice shall be undoubtedly destroyed.' Having thus spoken, Sati fixed her mind in profound abstraction, and by her own splendor consumed her body, while all the immortals exclaimed in astonishment, 'How wonderful!' On being informed of this event, Shiva, much afflicted, collected myriads of ghosts, goblins, and demons, and hastened to Daksha's place of sacrifice; which he completely destroyed, after having vanquished all the immortals that opposed him."

From the Skanda Puran, the Chapter entitled "Kapardi Mahatmyam."

GANESA CREATED.

Shiva, addressing Parvati: — "Formerly, during the twilight that intervened between the Dwapara and Kali Yugs, women, barbarians, Sudras, and other workers of sin, obtained entrance into heaven by visiting the celebrated temple of Someshwara. Sacrifices, ascetic practices, charitable gifts, and all the other prescribed ordinances ceased, and men thronged only to the temple of Shiva. Hence old and young, the skilled in the Vedas and those ignorant of them, and even women and Sudras, ascended to heaven, until at length it became crowded to excess. Then Indra and the gods, afflicted at being thus overcome by men, sought the protection of Shiva, and thus with reverence addressed him: 'O Shankara! by thy favor heaven is pervaded by men, and we are nearly expelled from it. These mortals wander wherever they please, exclaiming, "I am the greatest! I am the greatest!" and Dharma Rajah, beholding the register of their good and evil deeds, remains silent, lost in astonishment. For the seven hells were most assuredly intended for their reception; but, having visited thy shrine, their sins have been remitted, and they have obtained a most excellent futurity.' Shiva replied, 'Such was my promise to Soma, nor can it be infringed; and all men, therefore, who visit the temple of Someshwara must ascend to heaven. But supplicate Parvati, and she will contrive some means for extricating you from this distress.' The gods then kneeling before Parvati, with folded hands and bended heads, thus invoked her assistance with laudatory strains: 'Praise be to thee, O supreme of goddesses, supporter of the universe! Praise be to thee, O lotos-eyed, resplendent as gold! Praise be to thee, O beloved of Shiva, who createst and destroyest! Praise be to thee, O mountain-born! Praise be to thee, O Kalarattri, O Durga, who pervadest the universe, and art the sole substance from which all female forms, whether mortal or immortal, originate! Grant us thy aid, and save us from this fearful distress!' Having heard the supplication of Indra and the gods, thou, O goddess! wert moved with compassion, and, gently rubbing thy body, there was thence produced a wondrous being with four arms and the head of an elephant; when thou thus addressedst the gods: 'Desirous of your advantage have I created this being, who will occasion obstacles to men, and, deluding them, will deprive them of the wish to visit Somanatha and thus shall they fall into hell.' This heard, the gods

Ganesa.

The Hindu Serpent God.

Colossal Bust of Shiva at Elephanta.

Shiva

were delighted, and returned to their own abodes, relieved from all fear of mankind."

From the Lainga Puran, Part II., Chap. 100.

KALI CREATED.

Suta thus spoke:—"Formerly a female Asura,* named Daruka, had through devotion obtained such power, that she consumed like fire the gods and Brahmins. But, as she was attended by a numerous host of female Asuras, Vishnu, and all the gods, were afraid to engage in battle with her, lest they should incur the sin of *feminicide.* They in consequence proceeded to Shiva, and with laudatory strains entreated his assistance; and he then, regarding Devi, thus addressed her: 'Let me request, O lovely one! that thou wouldst now, for the benefit of the universe, effect the destruction of this Daruka.' Having heard these words, Parvati created from her own substance a maiden of black color, with matted locks, with an eye in her forehead, bearing in her hands a trident and a skull, of aspect terrible to behold, and arrayed in celestial garments and adorned with all kinds of ornaments. On beholding this terrific form of darkness, the gods retreated in alarm. Parvati then created innumerable ghosts, goblins, and demons; and, attended by these, Kali in obedience to her order, attacked and destroyed Daruka, and removed the distress of the world."

This legend concludes in the following singular manner: "Shiva also appeared as an infant in a cemetery surrounded by ghosts, and on beholding him Kali took him up, and, caressing him, gave him her breast. He sucked the nectareous fluid; but becoming angry, in order to divert and pacify him, Kali, clasping him to her bosom, danced with her attendant goblins and demons amongst the dead until he was pleased and delighted; while Vishnu, Brahma, Indra, and all the gods, bowing themselves, praised with laudatory strains the god of gods, Parvati and Kali."

From the Garura Puran.

INVOCATION TO DURGA, OR KALI.

"On the ninth of each half month invoke Durga with these words: '*Hrim, protect me, O Durga! O chief of the divine mothers! giver of blessings! accept these various offerings of flesh and my prayers.*' On the third, also, of Margashirsha commence

* Demon.

the worship of Durga before her image having eighteen hands, and holding in them a mace, a bell, a looking-glass, an iron rod, a bow, a banner, a small drum, a battle-axe, a noose, a lance, a club, a trident, a disk, a shield, an *ankush*, a dart, a thunderbolt, and a skull; and address to her the following hymn: 'Om, praise be to thee, O Bhagawati, Chamunda! dweller in cemeteries, bearer of a skull, borne on a car drawn by ghosts, Kalarattri, large-mouthed, many-armed, sounding thy bell and drum, laughing terribly, gnashing thy horrid teeth loudly, clothed in an elephant's skin, with a body full of flesh and blood, and a tremendous tongue! Praise be to thee, O Kali! with terrific tusks and fear-inspiring eyes flashing like lightning, with a countenance dark with frowns, bearing the moon on thy matted locks, and on thy neck a string of skulls! *Hram, Hram*, O destroyer of difficulties! quickly accomplish this business! O delighter in flesh and blood! be propitious, be propitious, and enter this place! Enter, enter! tread, tread! dance, dance! Why delayest thou to enter? O wearer of human heads and skulls! seize, seize! tear, tear! consume, consume! slay, slay! *Hrum, Hrum*, destroy, destroy! pierce, pierce with thy trident! kill, kill with thy thunderbolt! smite, smite with thy rod! cut off, cut off with thy disk! fell, fell with thy mace! strike, strike with thy axe! Come, come, O Maheshwari! come, O Kamarini! come, O Varahi! come, O Aindri! come, O Chamuṅda! come, O Kapalini! come, O Mahakali! come, O frequenter of Kailasa! enter, enter this place, O thou who executest the wrath of Rudra, and causest the destruction of the Asuras!'"

The Introduction or Dedication of the Mahabarat.

A HYMN OF PRAISE TO DURGA.

Hail, greatest of goddesses, victory unto thee,
Victory unto thee, Hurree Chandee!
In thy forehead thy red mark appeared so glowing,
O Dabee! we tremble to see thee.
At thy ears hang the gold rings so large and so brilliant;
At thy nose is the rich gapamatee;*
Thy hands hold the cleaver, and trident, and blood-dish—
So dreadful appears Bhagabattee!
Sixty-four times ten millions of witches and spectres,
Thee their patroness and mistress attending.
Thou art Loksmee, the primeval mother of all things,
In creation we see thee extending.

* Jewel.

In each house dost thou enter, on *holiness* thinking;
There to dwell with the pure thou art wont.
Fifteen million times than a warrior stronger,
Thine arm Moyassoor did slay;
Thy sword Roktabija, the dread demon, laid low,
And the fear of the gods did allay.
The wife of Eswara, a strange, fearful demon,
A ghost and the mother of all.
Nineteen millions of devils, all females and fearful,
From thy body came forth at thy call.
With round eyes and flat forehead thou starest portentious,
And utterest thy dread voice in thunder.
With thy cleaver and blood-dish and bloody tongue quivering,
Thou enterest graveyards, devouring choice corpses,
Still with battle-field slaughter unfilled.
How sweet is the blood of the good man unto thee!
Still his gore from thy mouth is distilled.
Thou rejoicest to hear the dread battle's loud slaughter,
The sound of the Ra! Ra! so dire.
The chief of the holy, thy names, lady, are many,
At the cry of Ra! Ra! swiftly flying.
Nine hundred times counted, one thousand of witches,
Of ghosts and of devils obey thee.
In the silence of midnight, when dark, are thy witches
A corpse for a vehicle using,
When the fresh dead are lying, thou a feast gladly makest,
With the green skulls thy fancy amusing.
When the flames of the funeral gleam through the night's darkness
When the dead they are wont to consume,
How swiftly thou runnest to snuff the rich odors!
To thee they are richest perfume.
To thy timbrel's jingle, in the air ever sounding,
Ghosts and devils innumerable dance;
They share in thy honors and share in thy worship,
As thy name and thy praise they advance.
Thou art greater than Brahma, or Vishnu, or Shiva
Thou art called the great Bhagabattee.

Translated by Rev. Charles Lacey, for Caleb Wright.

From the Matsya Puran, Chap. 3, 4.

BRAHMA'S INCEST.

"Brahma next formed from his own immaculate substance a female, who is celebrated under the names of *Shatarupa*, *Savitri*, *Sarasvati*, *Gayatri*, and *Brahmani*. Then, beholding his daughter, born from his own body, Brahma became wounded with the arrows of love, and exclaimed, 'How surpassing lovely she is!' But Shatarupa turned to the right side from his gaze, and, as Brahma wished to look after her, a second head appeared and thus, as she passed, in order to avoid his amorous glances, to his left and his rear, two other heads successively manifested themselves. At length she sprang into the sky, and, as Brahma was anxious to gaze after her, a fifth head was immediately formed. Then Brahma thus called to his daughter: 'Let us generate all kinds of animated beings, men, Suras, and Asuras.'* On hearing these words she descended; and, Brahma having espoused her, they withdrew into a secluded spot, and there indulged in the delights of love for one hundred divine years."

From the Vamana Puran, Chap. 6.

"Then Hara, wounded by the arrows of Kama, [the god of love,] wandered into a deep forest, named *Daruvanam*, where holy sages and their wives resided. The sages, on beholding Shiva, saluted him with bended heads, and he, wearied, said to them, 'Give me alms.' Thus he went begging round the different hermitages; and, wherever he came, the minds of the sages' wives, on seeing him, became disturbed and agitated with the pain of love, and all commenced to follow him. But, when the sages saw their holy dwellings thus deserted, they exclaimed, '*May the lingam of this man*† *fall to the ground!*' That instant the lingam of Shiva fell to the ground; and the god immediately disappeared. The lingam, then, as it fell, penetrated through the lower worlds, and increased in height until its top towered above the heavens. The earth quaked, and all things movable and immovable were agitated; on perceiving which, Brahma hastened to the Sea of Milk, and said to Vishnu, 'Say, why does the universe thus tremble?' Hari replied, 'On account of the falling of Shiva's lingam, in consequence of the curse of the holy and divine sages.' On hearing of this most wonderful event, Brahma said, 'Let us go and behold this lingam.' The two gods then repaired to Daruvanam; and, on beholding it without beginning or end, Vishnu mounted the king of birds and descended into the lower regions in order to ascertain its base; and, for the purpose of discovering its top, Brahma in a lotos car ascended the heavens. But they returned from their search wearied and disappointed, and together approaching the lingam, with due reverence and praises, entreated

* Suras are gods, and Asuras are demons.

† Shiva was disguised, and the sages, therefore, did not know him.

Shiva to resume his lingam. Thus propitiated, that god appeared in his own form, and said, 'If gods and men will worship * my lingam, I will resume it; but not otherwise.' To this proposal Vishnu, Brahma, and the gods, assented." †

From the Bhagavat Geeta, p. 90.

PART OF ARJOON'S DESCRIPTION OF KRISHNA, WHOM HE SAW IN A VISION.

"The winds, alike with me, are terrified to behold thy wondrous form gigantic; with many mouths and eyes; with many arms, and legs, and breasts; with many bellies, and with rows of dreadful teeth! Thus, as I see thee, touching the heavens, and shining with such glory, of such various hues, with widely-opened mouths, and bright, expanded eyes, I am disturbed within me; my resolution faileth me, O Vishnu! and I find no rest! Having beholden thy dreadful teeth, and gazed on thy countenance, — emblem of time's last fire, — I know not which way to turn! I find no peace! Have mercy, then, O god of gods! thou mansion of the universe! The sons of Dhreetarashtra now, with all those rulers of the land, Bheeshma, Drona, the son of Soot, and even the fronts of our army, seem to be precipitating themselves hastily into thy mouth, discovering such frightful rows of teeth! whilst some appear to stick between thy teeth with their bodies sorely mangled. As the rapid streams of full-flowing rivers roll on to meet the ocean's bed, even so these heroes of the human race rush on towards thy flaming mouths. As troops of insects, with

* It is now the principal object of worship in more than half of the temples of India.

† "The lingam is formed of stone, and consists of a base three or four feet high, the top of which is surrounded by a raised rim; and in the middle is slightly excavated, and raised on a level with the rim, the figure of a yoni, (*pudendum muliebre,*) from the centre of which rises a smooth, round stone, slightly conical towards the top, of a foot and a half in height and about three inches diameter at the base. Major Moor has, therefore, very justly observed, 'It is some comparative and negative praise to the Hindus, that the emblems under which they exhibit the elements and operations of nature are not externally indecorous. Unlike the abominable realities of Egypt and Greece, we see the phallic emblem in the Hindu Pantheon without offence; and know not, until the information be extorted, that we are contemplating a symbol whose prototype is indelicate. The plates of my book may be turned and examined over and over, and the uninformed observer will not be aware that in several of them he has viewed the typical representation of the generative organs or powers of humanity.'" — *Ancient and Hindu Mythology, by Col. Kennedy*, pp. 103, 104.

increasing speed, seek their own destruction in the flaming fire, even so these people, with swelling fury, seek their own destruction. Thou involvest and swallowest them altogether, even unto the last, with thy flaming mouths, whilst the whole is filled with thy glory, as thy awful beams, O Vishnu, shine forth on all sides!"

THE MOON PLANT SACRIFICE.

The moon-plant must be collected in a moonlight night, from the table-land on the top of a mountain, and carted to the place of sacrifice by two rams or he-goats. The juice of the plant, mixed with barley and other ingredients, becomes, by fermentation, a very intoxicating liquor. The officiating Brahmins are to drink this liquor as a part of the performance. The sacrifice continues several weeks, and is accompanied by numerous austerities which endanger the lives of the worshippers.

Tuka Rama, a sage who flourished about three hundred years ago, speaks of muzzling the animals used in carting the moon-plant, and of beating them to death by the fists of the Brahmins. His verses are to the following effect:—

"Beat to death the ram you've muzzled,
And offer the Soma with sacred song:—
So they say; but yet I'm puzzled,
And half suspect such worship wrong;
For rites like these are at best but scurvy,
That turn religion topsy-turvy."

In the Sama Veda, there is a series of about a thousand verses, designed to be chanted or sung at the moon-plant sacrifice. The following extracts will serve as specimens. Each paragraph, the last one excepted, contains an entire verse.

"O Agni! whether I now speak with true intonations or with false, I mean to praise thee. Come hither, therefore, and grow great by drinking this moon-plant juice."

"O Indra! drinker of the moon-plant juice, these thy friends [the attendant priests] look on thee, with the affection that the cattle-feeder looks on his cattle."

"We call on thee, the performer of meritorious acts, day by day, as men call on the cow to the milking."

"Let these moon-plants fill thee with delight, O holder of the thunderbolt! Do thou procure for us wealth, and, at the same time, kill outright all who hate the Brahmins."

"O Indra! wherever — whether in some strong chest or in some hill or well — treasure worthy of regard is laid up, thence do thou bring it to us."

"O Indra! this morning accept our sacrifice, accompanied with rice, curds, sweet cakes, and praises."

"Come into our presence to partake of the moon-plant juice and other viands. Do not get angry with us, [but bear with us] as an elderly man does with a young wife."

"We, who are eager for the possession of riches, take hold of thy right hand, O Indra, lord of wealth! We know thee, O mighty god! to be lord of cattle; give us then that wealth which consists in cows that yield large supplies of milk."

"O worthy of all praise! let our eucharistic songs fix thee, as firmly as the charioteer is fixed in his seat, and let their symphony sound before thee like the lowing of newly-calved cows for their calves."

"When, O Indra! those who come to worship invoke thee, and delight thee with sacrificial viands, and ceremonies used for the obtaining victory over our enemies, then do thou yoke thy banquet-going horses, and having slain some one, and seized his wealth, bestow it on us."

"Bestow on us a good and auspicious intellect, along with wisdom and food, that we may secure thy friendship; and do thou delight in our spirituous liquors as cows do in rich pasturage."

"He who causes the well-filled golden-colored horses' grain-dish to glisten, is the man who will stand in the first place before thy rain-causing, cow-conferring chariot. O Indra! now yoke thy horses."

"Come, O Indra! with all thy bands, like the herd of cows collected in the cow-house."

"The mountain-produced, pressed moon-plant is distilling its juice in the holy place. Thou, O Soma! art the embroiler of all things in thy drunken frolics."

"The Brahmins, void of malice, sing praises before the beloved, much-desired presence of Indra, with the affection cow-mothers lick their calves in the day they are produced."

"[O priests,] we praise all the day long that renowned, foe-destroying Indra of yours, who gets muzzy on the sacrificial beverage placed in the sacred vessels, with voices raised as loud as those of milch-cows lowing for their calves. [Indra,] we desire of thee quickly to give us food of heavenly origin, worthy of being bestowed, encircled with majesty as a mountain with clouds, capable of feeding multitudes, worthy of being extolled, in hundreds and thousands of different kinds of measure, and, united with it, abundance of cows."

"The sweet moon-plants, when pressed, flow in a stream, and with a loud voice, for the production of inebriation. The juices flow down during the time of bruising with a noise for the glorious toper Indra, who gives its splendor to the morning."

From the Padma Puran, Chap. IX.

OCCURRENCES IN THE HEAVEN KAILASA.

Narada said:—"At this time I went and informed Jalandhara that Shambhu * had promised to effect his destruction. Jalandhara then said to me, 'O holy sage! what precious things are contained in the abode of the bearer * of the trident? Acquaint me with the whole, as war should not be unless there be booty.' I replied, 'Shambhu is old, covered with ashes, his neck marked with the poison of serpents, mounted on a bull, bearing a beggar's dish in his hand, and with an elephant-headed and a six-headed son,† and he has nothing valuable belonging to him except the lovely and full-bosomed daughter of the mountain. Inflamed with love and captivated by her beauty, Mahesha * passes his days in sport and dalliance, or sings and dances to amuse her. She is named Parvati, and far excels in loveliness either Vrinda or the nymphs of heaven.' Having thus spoken, and excited the desire of Jalandhara, I disappeared.

"After this the son of the sea despatched Rahu on an embassy to Kailasa, who arrived there in a moment; and, on beholding the resplendent abode of Shambhu, he exclaimed to himself, 'How wonderful is this place!' He then wished to enter, but was prevented by the warders, who demanded his business. Rahu replied, 'I am the ambassador of Jalandhara; but the message of a mighty king is not addressed unto a doorkeeper.' Nandi, hearing these words, hastened and informed Shiva; and, having received his commands, introduced Rahu. Having entered, he beheld Shambhu, five-faced and ten-armed, his sacrificial cord formed of a snake, and his matted locks adorned with the moon, waited upon by vile and ugly servants, but attended

* Shiva.

† Ganesa and Kartika. See the engraving of Ganesa on page 21.

TEMPLE OF NANDI AT TANJORE

Nandi is the Bull on which Shiva is said to perform his journies. It appears from an extract from the Shasters commencing on the opposite page that Nandi is a quadruped of no ordinary attainments. His image in this temple is rudely carved from a large block of block granite.

by all the immortals, who, looking to the ambassador, desired him to speak. Rahu then began: 'O lord! I am sent to thee by Jalandhara: hear his auspicious words from my mouth; and do thou, who art addicted to devotion, devoid of affection, an abandoner of works, who hast neither father nor mother, nor observest the duties of the householder, obey his commands. The mighty Jalandhara enjoys the dominion of the three worlds; do thou also become subject to him. Why shouldst thou, old, libidinous, and the rider of a bull, refuse to obey him?' While Rahu thus spoke, the sons of Shiva, Ganesa and Skanda,* were rubbing his body; and, disturbed by their hands, Vasuki fell to the ground, and immediately began to swallow the rat, Ganesa's vehicle, beginning with the tail. Gananayaka,† on observing the snake about to swallow his courser, called out, 'Loose!

Skanda, or Kartika.

loose!' At this time Skanda's peacock began to scream in the shrillest manner; and the serpent, frightened, disgorged the rat, and hastened to replace himself on the neck of Shiva, where, violently respiring, he dimmed the brightness of the moon with his poisonous breath. Then came the beloved of Vishnu, dripping from her couch in the Milky Sea, and bearing a vase full with the beverage of immortality, with which she reanimated the head of Brahma that Shiva's hand eternally displays. The head, falling and rolling on the ground, exclaimed in boasting accents, while the spectators expressed to each other their astonishment, 'I am the first — I am the most ancient of beings — I am the creator — I am the lord of all things.' At this moment, from the matted locks of Shiva sprang myriads of beings, three-

* Kartika

† Ganesa.

faced, three-footed, seven-armed, and with yellow hair hanging in long and matted locks, on seeing whom the head became mute as the dead. Having beheld these wonders, Rahu, in fear and astonishment, thus again addressed Mahesha: 'O lord! through th strength of thy devotion and abstraction, affections touch not thee; why then dost thou sacrifice to feelings and passions? Thou receivest adoration from Brahma and all other deities; but who is the god whom thou adorest? Thou art the supreme god; why, therefore, dost thou collect the scraps of the beggar? But O chief of devotees! since thou preferrest a state of pious mortification, yield up Gauri and thy two sons, Ganesa and Skanda; and do thou, with a beggar's dish, wander from door to door.' Thus Rahu urged his request in many words; but Maheshwara returned no answer. Then Rahu, as Isha would not break silence, thus addressed Nandi: 'Thou art a minister and a general, and canst therefore inform me what means this departure from all received usages; as it is not becoming that a prince, to whom an ambassador is sent, should preserve silence.' But Nandi replied not, and immediately, on a sign from Shiva, reconducted and dismissed Rahu, who hastened to Jalandhara and related to him all that had passed."

"The mighty Jalandhara, having heard the relation of his ambassador, immediately arrayed his army and marched forward. Then the tumult of his approaching forces resounded through the inmost recesses of Mandara; and wide was it spread by the echoes of Meru, while lions started from their dens; warlike instruments with their clangor, dear to the warrior, deafened the three worlds; and, as trod the mighty Danavas, the lofty mountains trembled, and the seas were agitated. The armor of warriors clashed as on they marched, borne on various vehicles; and the wheels of the war-chariots harsh grated along the ground. White umbrellas shaded the mighty host from the sun, and fans formed of peacocks' feathers prevented heat. From the innumerable elephants, cars, horse, and foot, arose clouds of dust, which spread over the sky like the blue lotos, or the dark billows of the heaving ocean. * * * Then Nandi and Shumbha showered arrows on each other thick as the leaves are strown on Mandara when storms agitate its trees. At length Shumbha, throwing away his bow, rushed to the chariot of Nandi, and, wounding him on the breast, he fell senseless like a mountain struck by a thunderbolt."

EAST INDIAN CHARACTER AND CUSTOMS.

ILLUSTRATED BY ANECDOTES, ETC.

COMMUNICATED BY J STATHAM, A. M., OF HOWRAH, NEAR CALCUTTA

THE descendants of the Mohammedans who conquered India and established the Mogul Empire have become very numerous, and are scattered among the Hindu population throughout the entire peninsula. In their general appearance they resemble their pagan neighbors, and are not their superiors either in intelligence or in morality. I once met two rich Mohammedan merchants at the house of a ship-builder: they came in just after dinner, and readily took seats at the table. The gentleman of the house said, "I suppose it is of no use to offer you a glass of wine." "O, no, no, no!" they both replied; "the followers of the Prophet must drink no wine." Soon after this, one of them went out of the room, when the ship-builder, who seemed perfectly acquainted with the manœuvre, said to the other, "You had better taste the wine: come, help yourself." To my great surprise, the merchant took a tumbler, instead of a wine-glass, and, filling it to the brim, drank it off; the other soon returned, when his friend went out, and exactly the same occurred again: thus they could not accuse each other.

The principal festival of the Mohammedan population of India is the Mohurrum. It is celebrated with as much pomp and display as their circumstances will allow; and during the ten days which it continues, all the followers of the Prophet, of every rank and degree, are totally absorbed in its ceremonies. Different scenes are represented each day by means of effigies, gilded thrones, chariots, and various paraphernalia of royal and warlike pageants, attended by hosts of living actors, who manifest, at some periods of the festival, the most frantic grief, beating their breasts with great violence, and exclaiming, in rapid accents, "Oh Hussein Heif az Hussein." On the first day, their zeal and enthusiasm are excited by the addresses of the Moulahs, who harangue them on the incidents pertaining to the tragic history of Hussein, his brother Hassan, and their father Ali, of which the following is a brief sketch. Ali, the caliph, was beloved by his subjects, but fell by the hand of an assassin, and the regal power was usurped by his bitterest enemy, who failed in his design of murdering the young princes, Hussein and Hassan. When the usurper died, he was succeeded by his son Yezzed, during whose reign a plot was formed to restore the house of Ali to the throne, and trusty messengers were despatched to Medina to invite Hussein to invade the kingdom, and to assure him that the faithful were anxious to throw off the yoke of their tyrant, and acknowledge him as their rightful sovereign. The prince did not hesitate to comply with the invitation, and collecting a small army, headed them in person, taking his family with him. Yezzed, being informed of his movements, sent a large army to meet him, which, having taken a position between Hussein and the River Euphrates, entirely cut off his supply of water. The consequence was, that, without coming to action, most of his followers forsook him, and fled; so that, in a short time, he numbered only seventy-two persons in his train, most of these being relatives. Still, with this little band, Hussein performed the most extraordinary feats of valor; but on the tenth day of Mohurrum, they were entirely surrounded by ten thousand of Yezzed's troops, and every one cut in pieces, Asher, the infant son of Hussein, being butchered in his father's arms. The head of Hussein was carried to Damascus, and laid at the feet of Yezzed. By the harangues of the priests and the scenic representations, such as the horses of Hussein and his brother covered with gashes and stuck full of arrows, cimeters and turbans stained with blood, and pigeons (which carried the sad news to Medina) with their beaks clotted with gore, the minds of the spectators are often excited to a state of frenzy bordering on madness, when they sometimes inflict wounds upon themselves and others, and in some instances many have been slain. Those who are strict in the observance of this festival endure great privations by an almost total abstinence from water during the ten days which the Mohurrum continues. Vast sums are lavished upon the scenic representations, and the public mind is greatly demoralized by the revengeful and bloodthirsty feeling which are engendered.

The Mohammedans have no system of caste; yet their inter

course with Hindus has led them to imagine that they have, and this is often productive of much inconvenience in families where they are employed as servants. In India, servants are a heavy burden upon the mind, and a great tax upon the purse. Civil and military officers are obliged to support a number of attendants, who merely add to their splendor when in public, without being of the least use in the family, such as chobdars, sotaburdars, and hurkarus. These men carry silver wands before the palankeen of their master, and bear letters or messages from on person to another. All persons who make any pretensions tc gentility employ a khansammah or house steward, a dhurwhan or doorkeeper, an abdar or water cooler, a sherabdar or wine manager, six or eight khitmutgars or waiters at table, a sirdar-bearer and eight others to carry the palankeen, two or three bobajees or cooks, bheesties or water carriers, mhaters or sweepers, out-of-door servants, grooms, etc., etc., to a great number. Families in the middle rank of life are also obliged to keep a large number of servants. Even missionaries, who endeavor to do with as few as possible, are under the necessity of employing a bobajee, bearer, khitmutgar, mhater, dhurwhan, syce, grasscut, and dhobee or washerman. The salary of these averages about two dollars per month. Many families in the higher ranks of society have as many as a hundred or a hundred and twenty servants employed in their houses and gardens, none of whom are deemed superfluous.

Such a train of servants is a continual source of vexation. Those who have the management of the table will commit such petty thefts as to elude observation, but which, constantly repeated, amount to a heavy tax in the course of a year: for instance, I had a box of tea opened, from which I took four pounds, and sent it to a friend; in about two months, I wanted some for use, and then found that, instead of eight pounds, only two remained. Now, this theft had not been committed at one time, nor at twenty times, but daily; a small pinch had been taken every time the khitmutgar had access to the godown, so that its decrease had been, as it were, imperceptible. Being suspicious that such petty thefts were constantly carried on, I one night stopped the Mohammedan servants at the gate, as they were going home, and ordered them to pull off their cummerbunds, (girdles,) when my suspicions were fully realized: small quantities of salt, sugar, tea, spice, quills, and a desert knife, were carefully concealed in their folds. It would have been vain to have discharged them, as new servants would not only be a trouble until they became acquainted with the manners and customs of the family, but would most certainly follow the same plan. I therefore endeavored to make them ashamed, and threatened to stop the value of all the articles missed out of their joint wages, at the same time ordering the dhurwhan to search them whenever they left the premises.

Although they profess not to drink spirituous liquors, yet I found I could never leave any spirits in their way without the quantity being considerably lessened. A gentleman called in one day who wished for some brandy and water; I sent the servant to the cellaret to get the brandy, and when done with, to take it back: just after he had given me the keys and left the room, I heard a smash in the hall, and going to inquire the cause, the same servant said he was carrying a glass of water for one of the young gentlemen, but another, running against him, had knocked it out of his hand. I was turning on my heel to come away when a strong spirituous perfume caused me to suspect that the liquor spilled was brandy. One of the young gentlemen at the same moment putting his finger to it and tasting it, exclaimed, "It is brandy, sir, and not water." The man most positively asserted that it was nothing but water. "For which of the young gentlemen were you bringing it?" said I. "O! he had quite forgotten!" I then tasted it myself; and being thus convinced that it was brandy, I called for a candle, and lighting a piece of paper, threw it down, when the blue flame spread itself over the whole surface of the liquid; upon seeing which he, with the greatest effrontery and apparent astonishment, lifting up his hands, exclaimed, "You sahibs can do wonderful things—even make water burn!" The fact was, he had filled a large tumbler with brandy, and availing himself of the long flowing sleeve which covered his hand, he had brought it through the room when he gave me the keys.

For a long time, the silver spoons used o disappear very fast, although I took every precaution to insure their safety. The khansammah used to count them every night, and lock them in a drawer, then give me the key, and come for it in the morning to take them out. One night, I had the curiosity, after he had left, to open the drawer and count them myself, when I found that a tea and a desert spoon were deficient, although he had made them to appear correct. I immediately sent a hurkarrah to overtake him, and tell him I had something to say to him before he went to the bazaar in the morning, and that he had better come now, as I might not see him on the morrow. Accordingly, in a few minutes he came, when, although his cummerbund was taken off, the spoons were not found; but an old bearer, a Hindu who bore no good will to the khansammah, whispering, said "Examine his turban, sahib;" which I did, and there the spoons were found.

The bearer I have just mentioned was the best servant I ever had; yet he was not to be implicitly confided in: articles of clothing were constantly lost, and he knew nothing about them. One month, no less than six shirts, with several white jackets, had disappeared; but although he brought me clean clothes, and took charge of those which were put off, he could never account for the manner in which they were lost. At length, I made a list of all my wearing apparel, and counting them before him, gave him the keys of the wardrobe and the entire charge of them, stipulating that he should make good all deficiencies, at the same time giving him half a rupee per month additional to his wages, to enable him to meet any casualties that might happen; and the result was, that from that time I never lost any clothes.

The fawning, deceitful manners of the servants are calculated to lead Europeans to place the greatest confidence in them, until experience convinces them that not one word they say can be believed, or any reliance placed on a single promise they make. Lying is not considered a vice with them; but, on the contrary, the man who can dissimulate the most successfully is the most applauded, and the greatest lies, so far from being considered as worthy of censure, are extolled as a means of attaining the object sought. Hence I have known natives practise a well-organized system of deception for weeks in order to attain a comparatively trivial object.

On one occasion, I rode to the Botanical Gardens on horseback, and as the tide would serve to return, I preferred going back in a boat to riding my horse. I told the syce, therefore, to ride him home. This he positively refused to do, saying he could never think of presuming to sit on the horse which carried the sahib whose salt he ate; it was an honor he could not think of taking; no, he would lead the horse. As I did not wish to press the honor upon him, I told him to take his time and lead the horse gently home. I soon left the gardens in a bauleah belonging to a gentleman at Howrah, and landing at a ghaut a short distance from home, was walking thither, when who should come galloping along the road but my syce, evidently under the influence of liquor! He passed without recognizing me, as it was just dusk. I took no notice of the circumstance that night; but when I told him of it next day, he stoutly denied the fact, and it cost me a great deal of trouble to convince him that he had enjoyed the high honor of riding on the sahib's horse.

None of my servants would bring to table any kind of swine's flesh, saying that none but a mesaljie could handle the dishes in which it was placed. I humored them in this particular, and whenever bacon, ham, or a fat pig was brought to table, the mesaljie alone handed the dishes; and even the bearers went so far as to say that they could not pull the punkah (a large fan) whilst swine's flesh was upon the table. A captain of one of the Honorable Company's chartered vessels, dining with me one day, observed this, and told me that his servants had acted upon the same principles. "But the case is quite different now," said he, "for last week I had a ham boiled, and as usual, I was obliged to hire a man of low caste to wait at table. Having occasion to rise earlier the next morning than I generally do, I could not find a single servant; but hearing a hum of voices in the pantry, I looked in, and found all these servants, who had refused to bring the ham to the table, eating slices of it with pieces of bread and butter. Never did I witness greater consternation in any countenances than in theirs when they beheld me. 'O, ho! gentlemen,' said I, 'you cannot any longer refuse to bring ham upon the table, I should think; can you? I see how the land lies, and I shall ask a moonshee (Persian teacher) about it this morning.' 'O, sahib,' said they all, 'don't say a word about it, and we will do any thing you wish.' 'Very well,' said I, 'let me have no more bother about caste, and I will say nothing; but the first time that any demur is made, I will expose you all.' From that time," said he, "I have never heard a word about caste, and I dress swine's flesh almost every day."

Upon hearing this, it occurred to me that several of my hams had, after being dressed, disappeared very quickly: I therefore determined to take particular notice of the next, and in order to be certain whether the servants did partake of it or not, before it left the table I measured the joint unperceived by them, and when the ham made its appearance on the breakfast table the next morning, I applied the measure, and found a decrease of about three inches in the prime part. My suspicious being thus confirmed, I charged them with it; but they were all indignant at the idea. However, finding that I was confidently assured of the truth of the charge, rather than that I should dismiss them from my service, which I threatened to do if they made any demur about bringing swine's flesh to the table, they agreed to do it, provided all were obliged to share the disgrace. The same day, a friend sent me a very fine pig: it was dressed, and the whole host of servants, putting their hands to the dish, brought it in. From that time, my troubles on the score of caste ceased, but not so on the score of thefts. Three silver spoons being missed, suspicion fell on a Mohammedan lad; and the theft being proved against him, I sent him to the Thanna, thinking it no longer proper to pass these things over, as my forbearance only served to increase the evil. After he had been confined about a month, as I was going out one morning, his father and mother clamorously assailed me with demands for money, saying I had sent their boy to jail, from whose wages they had received one rupee eight annas per month; therefore, as an act of justice, I ought to allow them that sum for the time he had already been incarcerated, and in the same ratio for the time he might yet remain in prison. It was in vain that I spoke to them of the moral turpitude of their son's conduct; the only crime of which they considered him guilty was failing to escape detection. They waited constantly at the gates of my compound, and assailed me in the same manner whenever I went out. At length, finding that I would not comply with their demands, the old man offered to supply his son's place until his return from prison, and seemed greatly astonished when I told him that I could not think of receiving the boy into my service again. The old lady then became very abusive and insulting in her language, and I could hear her vociferations for a long time, as they passed up the village homeward.

A very large peepul tree, esteemed sacred by both Mohammedan and Hindu, spread its huge branches over a part of my compound, and so near the ground as to be very annoying to persons passing either on horseback or in a chaise. This tree was believed to be the residence of many spirits or peers, and was attended by an old fakeer of most wretched appearance and licentious manners, who received a large revenue from the celebrity of the tree and the consequent number of its worshippers. It was near the water side, being only separated from the beach by the public road, and a ghaut in front gave ready access to the wor shippers, of whom boat loads would arrive at all hours of the day and night from Calcutta to perform their devotions before it; and I never saw a native of any caste pass without salaaming to th tree. My upper windows completely overlooked the small hu in which the fakeer lived, and the space beneath the peepul, so that I had an opportunity of witnessing the gross deception practised by the fakeer towards the credulous worshippers. They generally brought clarified butter, sweetmeats, rice, and other viands, which were spread in form before the tree; and when this was done, and the prescribed prostrations made, they were required to go to the river and perform their ablutions; during which time some, and in most cases all, of the presents brought were conveyed into the fakeer's hut, who announced to the worshippers, on their return to the tree, that the peer had condescended to partake of the feast, and was well pleased with their offerings. I often remonstrated with him on the wickedness of his conduct, when he would, with the greatest effrontery, declare that the particular peer worshipped actually did eat the viands and that every night he held converse with several, whose spirits dwelt in the tree. This man was reported to be in league with a band of Dacoits who infested the river, and I have every reason to believe that he was the contriver and director of all their schemes. As I found the boughs of the tree increasingly troublesome, I told him that they must be trimmed; at which he flew into the most violent rage, and declared that, should I break only a twig off the sacred tree, my own blood would inevitably flow as the peer whose spirit dwelt in the particular branch woul execute the direst revenge upon me. He then told me some mos horrible tales of several Europeans who had cut or broken portions of the tree, and who had suffered the most dreadful agonies in consequence thereof before their deaths, which had alway occurred within a month of the time the transgression had beer committed. I told him it was in vain that he attempted to impose his idle tales upon me; I knew who had power to create and power to destroy, and was assured that the God I worshipped was the only living and true God; and to convince him that I did not fear his threats, I plucked a small branch of the tree beneath whose shade we were standing, at which he uttered a piercing scream, and retreated many paces from me, declaring that the vengeance of the peers would soon overtake me and was beginning a most vociferous tirade of abuse, when I stopped him short by threatening, if he thus continued, to immediately lop off every branch that overhung my premises, and called out for a hatchet. It was wonderful to behold the change this apparent determination effected: from the infuriate reviler he became the most abject suppliant; falling at my feet, and intermingling his petitions with the most fulsome praises, he besought me to have mercy upon him, for, should the tree be mangled in the least, the number of worshippers would diminish. I told him that I should be heartily glad of that, as he subsisted by fraud and deceit, and was the means of riveting the cruel fetters which bound the poor infatuated beings around him. At this juncture, a European friend, who had long been a resident in India, passed, and hearing the pleadings of the fakeer, to my great surprise most heartily seconded them, declaring his belief that it was dangerous to cut down the peepul tree, as he had heard of instances where those who had done so had died shortly afterwards. Some other reasons which he urged I thought more conclusive; but before I retired, I broke off another twig, to show him, as well as the fakeer, that I had no superstitious reverence for the tree, and told the latter that, unless the branches were so secured as not to interfere with those who passed beneath them, I should still carry my threat into effect. The next morning, I was waited upon by one of the richest Baboos in Calcutta, who most respectfully entreated me not to cut a single branch of the sacred peepul, promising that forthwith the boughs should be raised high enough to admit a free passage under them. This was accordingly done by ropes drawing them upwards, and stout posts supporting them from below. The reasons of my friend, which had weight with me, were these: The Honorable Company were averse to any acts of violence being used to the destruction of idolatrous usages, and probably, should I persevere, such an excitement would be produced by the influential natives as to call for the notice of government, and perhaps I should be sent from India on account of my rashness, (as it would no doubt be termed;) and even should this not be the case, such prejudices would be formed in the minds of the natives against me personally as to preclude all hopes of my usefulness in future. So the tree escaped. But from that time, I was much less annoyed by the nocturnal revels of its worshippers, as I made this a stipulation, that no bawling o beating of tomtoms should take place after bed time, and that my servants should not be reproached, as they had been, because they served one who did not reverence the tree.

It was not long after this that the fakeer was much mortified by a trick played on him by a young gentleman to whom he had been expatiating on the sanctity of the tree and the peers who dwelt in it. Amongst other stories, he told him that, on a certain day of the year, a peer was visibly seated on its topmost branch. It happened that, in a few days, a large monkey ascended the tree in quest of its berries, when this young gentleman ran to the fakeer, who was at some distance, and told him that he was very sorry that he had before doubted his word, for that he was now convinced of the truth of what he had told him, as he had just seen the peer in the top of the tree, and if he came he might see him too. The old man came in haste, wondering what he could mean, and earnestly gazing up into the tree, spied the monkey on its summit. This so completely chagrined him that he retired into his hut, and was not visible for many hours afterwards. Around this tree were hung many little earthen vessels containing water from the sacred Ganges for the peers to drink, and offerings of garlands or bouquets of flowers were daily suspended from its branches.

Many attempts were made by the fakeer and his associates to dislodge me from the house by stratagems and schemes which had taken effect with former residents; but they found I was proof against the fear of ghosts, though my servants were not. About forty young gentlemen were then residing with me; consequently the part of ghosts could not be acted, as formerly, without detection. One man, who was discovered in the act of imitating these nocturnal visitors, received a severe beating from one of my ushers, which probably had a great effect in preventing their tricks.

About three days before the commencement of the swinging festival, my syce came and solicited a fortnight's holiday. In answer to some inquiries which I made, he said that when his child was very ill, some months since, he had made a vow before the Brahmins that if the boy lived he would swing at the festival, and it was for the purpose of fulfilling his vow (the child having recovered) that he wished for the holidays. I told him that I could not for his own sake grant his request, and that, should he choose to be so foolish as to swing, it would cost him the loss of his place, as I never could tolerate such wanton cruelty. I then reasoned with him on the awful consequences of such superstitious practices, and directed his attention to the only means of obtaining the favor of God, or of making a propitiation for sin. The poor fellow left me much dejected, and went to inform the Brahmins of my refusal. They told him that, under the circumstances in which he was placed, the god would accept an offering instead of the performance of his vow: this was rated at five rupees, exactly the amount of one month's wages. He had just before received his pay, and disposed of it; so he came to me again, and besought me to give him five rupees in advance, that he might carry them to the Brahmins, who were waiting at the gate, having no doubt that I would cheerfully comply with wishes. His disappointment was apparently very great when told him that I certainly would not advance the money for any such purpose. After a long parley, finding that I was inexorable, he went to the Brahmins, and by my advice told them that he could not get the money then, neither should he ever be able to spare it for such ANECDOTES OF MONKEYS. :re many and loud. Amongst other curses, they declared that the child should die in a week, and the syce as well as myself in a few days afterwards. The poor fellow appeared very much alarmed during the whole of the next week, fearing the Brahminical curse would be verified. He was silent, dejected, and hardly able to perform his duties. As the week passed away without any symptoms of illness on the part of his child or himself, his vivacity returned; and about three weeks afterwards, when the servants received their wages, he said to me, "Sahib, I am much delighted that you prevented me from swinging; for now my back is not sore, my child is living and well, and what is best, (at the same time chinking the money just received,) the Brahmins have not eaten my rupees. Many salaams to you, Sahib; and for the future I shall never wish to swing." A long conversation ensued, which I hope was attended with good effect.

Sepoys, or native soldiers, when disciplined and commanded by European officers, are very courageous, attentive to the orders given, and strict in obeying them to the very letter. An officer of high rank, living in an elegant house in the midst of large leasure grounds, had a guard stationed on the premises, and a ntinel posted before the house. An order was given at the uard room, by the officer, that the sepoys on duty should permit no person, except his lady and children, to walk across the lawn out of the regular path. It was not long after this order was ssued before a sentinel observed the officer himself walking across he grass plat in front of the house, when he marched up to him, and declared that he must not walk there, as his orders were to let no person, except the lady and the children, pass that way. It was in vain that the officer told him that he was the command-r of the station, and that the order was issued by himself. The sepoy still persisted in declaring that his hookham was, that no person whatever, except the lady and children, was to promenade there; and the officer, smiling at the literal interpretation given by the sentinel, went to the guard room, and ordered that he him-elf might also have permission to cross the lawn. Another in-stance occurred at the hospital at Dinapore. At a time when great mortality prevailed, a sentinel was posted at the entrance of the dead room, where the bodies are placed as soon as life is extinct, and amongst other orders, he was directed not to let the bodies be taken away during the night. It so happened that a young man had fallen into a sort of trance, which had been mis-taken for death, and had, during the evening, been removed to the dead house. In the course of the night, he recovered so far as to know the situation in which he was placed, and summoning all his strength, he came to the door, with an intention of cross-ing the court to the hospital; but not without being perceived by the sentinel, who, although he was evidently much alarmed, yet declared that his hookham was, that no dead man should go from the place that night, therefore he must go back; and on he young man's attempting to pass by him, he very deliberately carried him back, and fastened the door. When the relief guard came, he reported that a dead man wished to come out, but that he detained him, according to his orders. The corporal imme-diately opened the door, and taking him up in his arms, carried nim to a bed in the hospital, and then summoned the steward to his aid, when, by proper treatment, the youth recovered, and was in a short time able to perform his duties as before, after having been literally numbered with the dead.

In visiting some of the Hindu temples, I have been disgusted with the worship paid to monkeys. I was about to enter the court of a large temple at Nuddea, when the officiating Brahmin said, "No person may visit the court of Huneman with his shoes on." I reasoned with him through a friend, who understood his language better than myself, and he became very abusive; but at length, after bearing his attack with calmness and composure, we were permitted to enter. He requested us to make an offering to the monkeys, either of fruit or sweetmeats, plenty of which were for sale at the gates of the enclosure; but this we declined.

The Ramauna festival is annually celebrated with great pomp, when Huneman, the monkey son of the god Pavana, who presides over the winds, is personified by some stout fellow, equipped with a mask and tail like a monkey, who, attended by an army of similar masks and tails, attacks the castle of the giant Ravana, to deliver Seeta, a princess who has been stolen away by the giant and his evil spirits from her husband, Rama Chandra; a fruitless attempt having before been made by her husband and his brother, Luchmunu, to effect her rescue. Formerly the youths who personified Rama Chandra, Luchmunu, and Seeta were afterwards sacrificed to the parties they had represented; but this part of the performance has long since been discontinued.

During the fruit seasons, I was much annoyed by monkeys: a whole tribe of the large species, called *ring-tailed*, came in from the jungles, and devoured all the fruit they could seize. When erect, they were as high as a common-sized man; and the agility which they displayed was truly astonishing. Behind my premises there was a long building formerly used as a rope walk, the flat roof of which was their favorite place of resort to gambol and chatter. When a European approached the spot, they would instantly ascend to the top of some almond trees in their vicinity; but if a native came quite near to them, they took no more notice of him than if he had been one of their own species.

One of these monkeys became quite familiar with the shopkeepers in the bazaar, and would help himself plentifully to rice, fruits, &c. I was much amused, one day, to hear a sweetmeat merchant thus expostulate with him: "My brother, you know I am a poor man; do not take my sweetmeat balls; take them from other shops: there is a rich man over the way; he has plenty of rupees; go to him. Nay, nay, brother, that is too bad," (the monkey having just crammed a great ball of sweetmeat into his jaws ;) "I cannot afford so much : indeed, my brother, I cannot.' And the poor shopkeeper, apparently very much against his inclination, used a bamboo to guard his property. .The same animal played me a trick soon after, that might have proved of serious consequence. I was riding through the bazaar on horseback, when he caught hold of my horse's tail, and began to pull first to one side and then to the other. I had no whip, and he was a long-armed, powerful creature : the horse struck at him, but he maintained his hold without being kicked ; and in this manner we proceeded a considerable distance, the horse becoming more violent in his kicking and rearing, and the monkey more active in his pulling, until my syce, having procured a bamboo, assailed the enemy in the rear, when he took refuge on the roof of a banyan's shop. I have seen these monkeys seize the sacred ox by the tail, and give it a sudden and powerful twist, when he would run off at a full gallop, roaring with pain and fright.

A friend, whose premises adjoined mine, had a litter of pigs in a sty raised upon posts, to secure it from the attacks of jackals and foxes, but it was not out of the reach of monkeys. Hearing an unusually loud and uproarious commotion in this elevated habitation of little grunters, we hastened to ascertain the cause, and found that a monkey had seated himself astride the mother, and with one of her ears firmly grasped in each hand, was riding in fine style around the sty. The servants shouted, and he made his retreat, but not without taking with him one of the offspring of his nag. Holding it by the hind legs, he mounted to the top of a tall cocoa-nut tree, and then very deliberately placed his prisoner under his arm, and began to turn its tail round and round, as music-grinders turn the handle of the hand organ ; and at every turn this living instrument of music sent forth loud and piercing notes, which were responded to in various tones from the sty. The servants began to pelt him with stones, which caused him to leap from tree to tree; but finding himself embarrassed by the weight he carried, he threw the pig into the air, and as it fell fifty or sixty feet, it was instantly killed. .

These monkeys became so audacious that it was unsafe to leave any thing portable about the premises. A very large dog, belonging to a gentleman in the neighborhood, used occasionally to give chase to any of them that he found alone at a distance from the trees ; but one day, as he was running after a small one that came own to the river side, three large ones left the trees to attack nim. First one and then another would lay hold of his tail, and swing him around, then, grasping his neck, bite his ears; and in consequence of the great length of their arms, it was in vain that he attempted to retaliate. One of them at length grasped his throat so tightly that, in a short time, he would have been killed, had I not gone to his rescue. Taking a gun in my hand, I went towards the scene of action, and in a moment the monkeys were far enough away; but the poor dog was so terribly bitten, that for many days it appeared improbable that he would recover; and when able to run about again, we never could induce him to chase a monkey.

One morning, a little boy, about eight years of age, was going to school with a bunch of plantains in his hand, to be eaten at tiffin: these did not escape the watchful eye of a large monkey perched upon an almond tree near the road. Making a rapid though circuitous movement to gain the rear, Jackoo soon came up with the object of his pursuit, and jumping between the bearer and the boy, he put his long arms around the child's neck, and seized the plantains. The bearer screamed, and fled to a distance; but the child, though terribly alarmed, maintained his fights manfully for a considerable time, clinging to his plantains with all his might: but Jackoo was not to be disappointed; giving the boy a blow on the head, he knocked him down, and bore off the plantains in triumph.

The propensity of the monkey to retain whatever he grasps is often taken advantage of to capture him. Two large bunches of plantains are put into two narrow-necked jars, and placed where they will attract his attention. He eagerly seizes the plantains, but soon finds that he cannot extricate his hand, yet will not let go his hold, and will endeavor to make his escape with the jars and their contents, but at a very slow pace, as, both his hands being thus secured, he is obliged to shuffle along in an erect posture. When pursued, he will still maintain his hold, screaming, grinning, and chattering until he is secured by throwing a noose over his head.

In the course of a journey on the Ganges, my boat stopped for the night in the vicinity of Nuddea, and I happened to stroll into a bamboo tope, or jungle. I had not proceeded far before I heard a great uproar around me; and as I looked up, I saw a great multitude of large monkeys advancing toward me from every direction. Some leaped upon the ground before me, others swung by the bamboos over my head, and many closed up the path in the rear. Several of the females had their young clinging to them; but this did not seem to render them less agile than the others. A few of the largest, and apparently the oldest, chattered together a moment, and then the whole tribe responded, and advanced towards me. What to do I knew not: however, I hallooed as loud as I could, to make my people hear, and the monkeys retreated a few paces. This encouraged me to persevere; but I perceived that, when I began to retreat, they closed upon me again, without being at all affected by my noise. Once more I stood still, and gave a tremendous shout, when back they went again. I gained at least twenty yards, at that time, before they returned; and just as I was about to commence another shout, I saw a decrepit old woman hobbling through the midst of them. They appeared to be very familiar with her, and she shook several by the paw as she passed them. As soon as she had approached near enough to me to be heard, she poured out a torrent of abuse against me for disturbing the sacred animals in their retirement, and motioned me, with almost frantic gestures, to depart quickly, her tongue never ceasing till I was quite out of hearing. I was not long in complying, as the monkeys seemed implicitly to obey her, and cleared the path by which I could retreat. In returning to the boat, I met my servant, who said that he was coming to tell me not to disturb the monkeys in the bamboo grove, for it belonged to Huneman. The people throughout the country worshipped them, and brought them offerings of rice and sweetmeats, and the old woman was employed to feed them.

The jackals of India, which are exceedingly numerous, are very useful in devouring offal, the carcasses of dead animals, and the corpses floated ashore upon the banks of rivers; yet their depredations, and their dismal howlings at night, are more than equivalent to their usefulness as scavengers. Soon as the busy hum of the bazaars and streets is ended, and all nature seems about to take repose, their barking or howling commences. Whilst sitting in the verandah to enjoy the evening breeze, you hear the well-known cry,—perhaps a solitary howl from a jackal at a great distance,—and you are glad that it is no nearer; but before your self-gratulations are completed, probably five or six, or even ten, of these clarion-tongued mourners open their cry simultaneously, close by the spot where you are sitting, and the sound thrills through every nerve. Then silence succeeds for a few minutes, when their cries again break forth in another quarter, and it seems as if an army of them was spread over all the country, as in every direction the same cries are heard; and woe be to any domestic fowl, kid, lamb, or rabbit that is not well secured by high walls and safely-fastened doors. A few years since, one of the up-country rajahs paid a visit to the governor-general; and as he came by the great Benares road, he left all his retinue at Howrah, instead of taking them over the river to Calcutta. Some of the elephants and camels were much jaded by the fatigues of the journey, so much so that one of the largest elephants died, and the rajah ordered it to be buried in a plain at a little distance. An immense grave was dug, and the unwieldy beast was, by the help of the other elephants, drawn to the place, and rolled into the yawning gulf below. It was a very interesting spectacle, as the surviving elephants seemed to mourn its loss, and I could see the tears trickle down their cheeks in fast succession, as they paid this last friendly office to their deceased companion. The animal must have weighed many tons, and it could not have been carried to the grave but by the help of these sagacious creatures. Notwithstanding the hole was dug so deep as to allow six feet of earth above the body of the elephant, the jackals began their ravages, and in a very few days more than a hundred of them were feasting upon the carcass.

The elephant is a valuable auxiliary to government in transporting stores and troops to the different stations where no water conveyance is available. A gentleman, being about to travel to a distant station, had many government elephants put under his care; and they were brought over to Gusserah to wait his departure. As he was staying with a friend of mine, I cheerfully complied with his request that the elephants might remain beneath a shady grove of mangoes in my large compound. There I had a constant opportunity of watching their movements, and was delighted and surprised in witnessing their sagacity and docility. Every morning, they came down to the river side to wash. Lying upon one side in the stream, each elephant would fill its trunk with water, and squirt it over the place where the mohout was rubbing; then, kneeling, would perform the same operation on its back; and lastly on the other side, until the whole body was cleansed. One of these animals, in passing through the bazaar, suddenly came upon a man sleeping in the path; when, rather than crush him beneath its foot, the careful animal rolled him over with its trunk, and placed him out of danger. The man awoke in a terrible state of alarm; but the elephant acted with the greatest coolness and caution. Whenever a branch of a tree hangs in the way of the howdah, although the elephant itself might pass under it, yet, knowing it would incommode its master, the considerate beast seizes it, and rends it off, that no inconvenience may be sustained by its rider. Whenever an elephant scents a tiger, which it can do at a considerable distance, it utters a shrill cry, and elevates its trunk perpendicularly to repel the attack. The leaps which the tiger makes in its charge are truly astonishing; yet a well-trained elephant will generally succeed in repelling the most furious attack, by dashing the springing tiger to the earth with its trunk; when, if its foe be at all stunned or maimed by the fall, or wounded by the rifle of the sportsman, the ponderous foot of the mighty beast will crush the fallen victim, and complete its destruction. But, in most instances, a well-directed ball stops the career of the tiger before he reaches the point of attack. When an elephant turns from the contest, the life of its rider is in danger, as the tiger can easily climb up in the rear, and seize the person in the howdah before he can turn to defend himself. A few years since, a party of Europeans, consisting of indigo planters and some of the officers of a native regiment stationed in their neighborhood, went into the jungles for the purpose of shooting tigers, and had not proceeded far before they roused an immense tigress, which, with the greatest intrepidity, charged the line of elephants on which they were seated, when a female elephant, in the direct point of attack, which had been lately purchased, and was hitherto untried, turned suddenly around, to fly from the field of battle, showing the greatest dread of the approaching foe. The tigress instantly sprang upon her back, and seizing the gentleman in the howdah by the thigh, brought him to the ground; then, throwing him, stunned by the fall, over her shoulder, just as a fox carries a goose, she started off into the jungle. Every rifle was pointed at her, but no one dared to fire on account of the position in which her captive lay.

She went through the jungle grass much faster than the elephants could, and was soon out of sight; but her pursuers were enabled to trace her by the blood in her track; and as a forlorn hope, they resolved still to follow on, to see if it were possible to save the remains of their friend from being devoured. As they proceeded, the traces grew fainter and fainter, until, at length, bewildered in the heart of the jungle, they were about to give up the pursuit, when they came unexpectedly upon the tigress, lying dead upon the long jungle grass, still griping the thigh of their associate in her tremendous jaws, whilst he, though still sensible, was unable to speak. To extricate him was impossible without first cutting off the head of the tigress, which was immediately done, and the jaws being severed, the fangs were drawn out of the wounds; and as one of the party providentially happened to be a surgeon, the patient was properly attended to, and the party had the satisfaction of returning with their friend, rescued from a most perilous situation, and with hopes of his recovery. He was taken to the nearest bungalowe, and by the aid there afforded, he was in a short time able to see his friends, and to explain how it was that the animal was thus found dead. For some time after the beast had seized him, he continued insensible, being stunned by the fall. When he came to himself, he discovered that he was lying on the back of the tigress, who was trotting along, at a rapid pace, through the jungle; and every now and then, his face and hands would receive the most violent scratches from the thorns and bushes through which she dragged him. He gave himself up as lost, and determined to lie quietly on her back, waiting the issue, when it occurred to him that he had a pair of pistols in his girdle, with which he might yet destroy his captor. After several ineffectual attempts, he at length succeeded in drawing one from the belt, and directing it at the creature's head, he fired; but the only effect which it seemed to produce was to cause her to quicken her pace, and to give him an angry shake, by which she made her fangs meet more closely in his flesh. From the excruciating pain thus produced he fainted, and remained totally unconscious of what was passing for some time, when, recovering a little, he determined to try the effect of another shot in a different place; so, getting the remaining pistol out of his girdle, he pointed the muzzle under the blade bone of the shoulder, in the direction of the heart, and once more fired, when the tigress fell instantly dead, and neither howled nor struggled after she fell; neither had he the power to call for aid, though he heard his friends approaching, and was fearful that they might pass the spot without discovering where he lay. The wounds healed, but the sinews of the limb were so dreadfully lacerated that he never entirely recovered the use of it.

In the Morung forests, at one season of the year, many persons are employed in cutting saul timber. I was assured by a friend, who had for years employed a great number of these persons, that when a tiger is found to be near where they are at work, one of the party, in a state of nudity excepting a girdle around his waist, which is filled with small pebbles, approaches the lair of the beast on all fours, making a peculiarly hideous noise, using the most extravagant gestures, and occasionally casting a few of the pebbles at the tiger, who views the strange figure with evident marks of trepidation, and slinks back from his approach. The gestures of the man now become more violent, and being accompanied by a copious discharge of pebbles and a still more hideous shout, the affrighted animal makes a hasty retreat. A signal being given, the whole band of workmen join in a continued cry, until the trembling brute is far beyond the reach of its supposed pursuer. The men engaged in this employment have no hesitation in going into the most wild and lonely jungles, as this method of frightening away wild beasts was never known to fail.

The following incident will serve to show the danger to which the inhabitants of India are continually exposed from serpents. A gentleman was one evening writing a letter, while his left arm was carelessly hanging over the side of the table, when a friend, who sat by him, said, "Mr. B., don't move a muscle upon any consideration; for a cobra di capello is surveying your hand, and the least movement will cause it to snap at you." The gentleman glanced his eye round, and, sure enough, there was the snake dancing its head round and round his hand. With the greatest self-possession, he maintained his position. At length, the snake, poking its head into the sleeve of the gentleman's white jacket, began to ascend his arm; still not a muscle moved, not a feature was altered: soon the reptile emerged from the sleeve at the collar, when the movement of his friend, alarming it, caused it to descend his back to the ground, where it was soon killed.

Had not the gentleman manifested this self-possession, he would have alarmed the snake, which, for self-defence, would no doubt have seized the object of its terror.

The whip snake is another venomous and most dangerous reptile. Its body is long and slender, very much in size like the thong of a chaise whip, from which I suppose it derives its name. This snake frequents the trees, and, fixing its tail round a branch will dart forward its whole length to seize any object that may unconscious of the danger, pass below it. One evening, whilst walking beneath a small mango tope, I felt a smart rap upon the crown of my hat, and looking up, saw one of these reptiles darting from the bough just above my head: with great difficulty I managed to destroy it, but not before I had sent for my gun and shot at it several times.

EAST INDIAN CHARACTER AND CUSTOMS,

ILLUSTRATED BY ANECDOTES, ETC.

COMMUNICATED BY AN ENGLISH LADY RESIDING IN INDIA.

We have just arrived in India, and are at our cousin Stanton's house at Madras. The scene in the Madras roads is the brightest and liveliest possible. The sea is completely studded with ships and boats of every size and shape, and the boats are manned with crews even more quaint and picturesque than themselves. But none can compare with the catamarans, and the wonderful people that manage them. Fancy a raft of only three logs of wood, tied together at each end when they go out to sea, and antied and left to dry on the beach when they come in again. Each catamaran has one, two, or three men to manage it: they sit crouched upon their heels, throwing their paddles about very dexterously, but in a manner remarkably unlike rowing. In one of the early Indian voyagers' log-books is the following entry respecting a catamaran: "This morning, 6, A. M., saw distinctly two black devils playing at single-stick. We watched these infernal imps above an hour, when they were lost in the distance. Surely this doth portend some great tempest." It is very curious to watch these catamarans putting out to sea. They get through the fiercest surf, sometimes dancing at their ease on the top of the waves, sometimes hidden under the waters; sometimes the man completely washed off his catamaran, and man floating one way and catamaran another, till they seem to catch each other again by magic.

I have seen so many curiosities already that I do not know which to describe to you first — jugglers, tumblers, snake-charmers, native visitors, &c., &c. For the last few days we have been in a constant bustle. Those snake-charmers are most wonderful. One day, we had eight cobras and three other snakes all dancing round us at once, and the snake-men singing and playing to them on a kind of bagpipe. The venomous snakes they call *good* snakes: one, the Brahminee cobra, they said was so good, that his bite would kill a man in three hours; but of course all these had their fangs extracted. The men bring them in covered baskets. They place their baskets on the ground, and play their bagpipes for a while; then they blow at the snakes through the baskets; then play a little more; at last, they take off the lid of the baskets, and the snake rises up, arching his neck like a swan, and with his hood spread, looking very handsome, but very wicked.

We have had a great many visits from natives to welcome A back again, or, as they say, "to see the light of master's countenance, and bless God for the honor!" One—a gentleman, in his black way—called at six in the morning; he left his carriage at the gate, and his slippers under a tree; and then, finding that we were going out riding, he walked barefoot in the dust by the side of our horses till "our honors" were pleased to dismiss him. Another met us, got out of his carriage, thrust off his shoes, and stood bowing in the dirt while we passed; then drove on to the house, and waited under the verandah for an hour and a half, till we were pleased to finish our ride. One paid me a visit alone, and took the opportunity to give me a great deal of friendly advice concerning managing A. He especially counselled me to "persuade him *to tell a few lies.*" He said he had often advised "master" to do so; but that he would not mind *him*, but "perhaps mistress persuade master. Master very good—very upright man; he always good; but master say all same way that he think. Much better not! Mistress, please tell master. Any body say wrong, master's mind different: that quite right—master keep his own mind; his mind always good: but let master say all same what others say; that much better, and they give him fine appointment, and plenty much rupees!" I said that that was not English fashion; but my visitor assured me that there were "plenty many" Englishmen who told as many lies as the natives, and were all rich in consequence: so then I could only say it was very wrong, and not master's fashion, nor mine; to which he agreed, but thought it "plenty great pity"!

These natives are a cringing set, and behave to us English as if they were the dust under our feet; and indeed we give them reason to suppose that we consider them as such. Their servility is disagreeable, but the rudeness and contempt with which the English treat them are quite painful to witness. Civility to servants, especially, seems a complete characteristic of *griffinage.* (A griffin is a fresh man or fresh woman in India.) One day, I said to my ayah, (a very elegant lady in white muslin,) "Ayah, bring me a glass of toast and water, if you please." She crept to the door, and then came back again, looking extremely perplexed, and whined out, "What mistress tell? I don't know." "I told you to bring me some toast and water." "Toast water I know very well, but mistress tell *if you please;* I don't know *if you please.*" I believe the phrase had never before been addressed to her. Every thing seems to be done by means of constantly finding fault: if one lets the people suppose they have given a moment's satisfaction, they begin to reason: "Master tell very good; try a little more than worse; perhaps master like plenty as well." One day, I gave some embroidery to be done by a Moorman recommended by my tailor: the Moorman did not bring his work home in time; I asked Mrs. Stanton what was to be done. "O," she said, "of course stop the tailor's pay." "But it is no fault of the poor tailor's." "O, never mind that; he is the Moorman's particular friend, and he will go and beat him every day till he brings the work home."

They are like babies in their ways. Fancy my great fat ayah, forty years old, amusing herself with puffing the wind in and out of my air-cushion till she has broken the screw! The jargon that the English speak to the natives is most absurd. I call it "John Company's English," which rather offends Mrs. Stanton. It seems so silly and childish, that I really cannot yet bring myself to make use of it; but I fancy I must in time, for the king's English is another characteristic of *griffinage,* and the servants seem unable to understand the most common direction till it is translated into gibberish.

A moonshee seems to be a component part of most English establishments; so I have set up one also. He comes three times a week to teach me Tamul. He is a very solemn sort of person, with long mustachios, and numbers of beautiful shawls, which he twists round his waist till they stand out half a yard in front of him, and come into the room before his face appears. When we hired him, he made many salaams, and said he preferred our friendship to any remuneration we could give; but he condescends to accept five pagodas a month besides. He comes when I choose, and goes away when I bid him. If I am not ready, he sits on his heels in the verandah for a couple of hours, doing nothing, till I call him. If I am weary in the course of my lesson, I walk away, and bid him write a little; and there he sits, scribbling very slowly and very intently, till I please to come back again. He is president of a Hindu literary society, and at its first opening delivered a lecture in English, of which he is very proud. He brought it to me to-day to read. The whole was capital; and it concluded with a hope "that this respectable institution, so happily begun in smoke, might end in blaze"! This Tamul that he is to teach me is a fearfully ugly language—clattering, twittering, chirping, sputtering, like a whole poultry-yard let loose upon one; and not a singing-bird, not a melodious sound among them. I suspect that I shall soon grow tired of it; but meanwhile it is a little amusement. A Tamul writer came to-day to copy some document on cadjan-leaf for Mr. Staunton. He held the leaf in one hand, and a sharp steel-pointed style, for a pen, in the other. He wrote very fast, and seemed quite at his ease, though sitting on his heels, and writing on his hand in this inconvenient manner.

Few things amuse me more than the letters we daily receive from natives, underlings in office, who knew A. before he went to England. One apologizes for troubling him with "looking at the handwriting of such a remote individual," but begs leave humbly to congratulate him on the safe arrival in India of himself and his "respectable family"—meaning me! Another hopes soon to have the honor of throwing himself at "your goodness's philanthropic feet." Is not this the true Fudge style?

The other day, a very rich native, an old *protégé* of A.'s, came to say that he and his son wished to make a feast for me, if I would come to their house. I was extremely glad, for I was longing to get into one of the native houses; so we accepted the invitation. Armagum and Looboo, our two entertainers, met us at their garden gate with lanterns, and rows of natives extended all the way up to the house, which was lighted up most brilliantly with innumerable chandeliers, lamps, and lustres, hung from the ceiling and festooned to the walls. The house consisted of one very large verandah, that opened into a large drawing room, with a smaller room at each end, and sleeping rooms beyond; and on the other side of the drawing room another verandah, leading into another garden. The house was furnished very much like a French lodging house, only with more comfortable ottomans and sofas; but the general effect was very French; quantities of French knickknacks set out upon different tables, and the walls quite covered with looking glasses.

We were led into the great drawing room, and seated upon sofas, and servants were stationed at our side to fan us. Armagum and Looboo brought us each a nosegay of roses, and poured rose water over them and over our hands; and they gave me a queer kind of sprig, made of rice and beads, like a twelfth-cake ornament. They also gave us each a garland of scented flowers, so powerful that even now, at the end of the next day, I cannot ged rid of the perfume on my hands and arms. Then the entertainment began. They had procured the musicians, dancers, and cooks belonging to the nabob, in order that I might see all the Mussulman amusements, as well as those of the Hindus. First came in an old man with a long white beard, to play and sing to the vina, an instrument like a large mandolin, very pretty and antique to look at, but not much to hear. His music was miserable, just a mixture of twang and whine, and quite monotonous, without even a pretence to a tune. When we were quite tired of him, he was dismissed, and the nabob's dancing girls came in — most graceful creatures, walking, or rather sailing about, like queens, with long muslin robes from their throats to their feet. They were covered with gold and jewels, ear rings, nose rings, bracelets, armlets, anklets, bands round their heads, and rings on all their fingers and on all their toes. Their dancing consisted of sailing about, waving their hands, turning slowly round and round, and bending from side to side. The prettiest of their performances was their beautiful swan-like march. Then they sang, bawling like bad street singers — a most fearful noise, and no tune. Then we had a concert of orchestra music, with different looking instruments, but in tone like every modification of bagpipes — every variety of drone and squeak; you can form no idea of such sounds under the name of music: the chimney sweepers' clatter on May day would be harmonious in comparison. Imagine a succession of unresolved discords, selected at random, and played on twenty or thirty loud instruments, all out of tune in themselves and with each other, and you will have a fair idea of Hindu music and its effect on the nerves.

When my teeth had been set on edge till I could really bear it n longer, I was obliged to beg A. to give the musicians a hint t stop. Then there came in a man to imitate the noises of various birds. This sounded promising, but unfortunately the Madras birds are screaming, and not singing birds; and my ears were assailed by screech owls, crows, parrots, peacocks, &c., so well imitated that I was again obliged to beg relief from such torture. Then we had a Hindu dancing girl, decorated with the most magnificent jewelry I ever saw: her dancing was very much like that of the Mohammedans, only a little more difficult. There was a good deal of running backwards and forwards upon her heels, and shaking her silver bangles or armlets, which jingled like bells; then glissading up to me, waving her pretty little hands, and making a number of graceful, unmeaning antics, with her eyes fixed on mine with a strange, unnatural stare.

After her performance was ended, we had a conjurer, some of whose tricks were quite marvellous. He had on a turban and a cummerbund, (or piece of muslin wrapped round him,) but no jacket, so that one could not imagine a possibility of his concealing any of his apparatus about him; but, among other tricks, he took a small twig of a tree, ran his fingers down it to strip the leaves off,—small leaves, like those of a sensitive plant,—and showered down among us, with the leaves, five or six living scorpions; not little things like Italian scorpions, but formidable animals, almost as long as my hand. I did not admire their company, creeping about the room; so he crumpled them up in his hand, and they disappeared. Then he waved his bare arms in the air, and threw a live cobra into the midst of us. Most of his other tricks were juggling with cups and balls, &c., like any English conjurer; but the scorpions and cobra were quite beyond my comprehension.

After he was dismissed, we had another gold and silver girl, to dance upon sharp swords, to music as sharp; then a fire eater; and, last of all, a great supper laid out in the back verandah. The first course consisted of all the nabob's favorite dishes of meat, and curries, and pillaws, set out in China plates; the second course consisted of Hindu cookery, set out in cups and saucers. A. whispered to me that I must eat as much as I could, to please poor old Armagum; so I did my best, till I was almost choked with cayenne pepper. The Moorman pillaws were very good;

but among the Hindu messes I at last came to something so queer, slimy, and oily, that I was obliged to stop.

After supper, Armagum made a speech, to inform me that he was aware that the Hindus did not know how to treat ladies; that he had therefore been that morning to consult an English friend of his concerning the proper mode of showing me the respect that was my due; and that he had informed him that English ladies were accustomed to exactly the same respect as if they were gentlemen, and that he had better behave to me accordingly. He begged I would consider that, if there had been any deficiency, it was owing to ignorance, and not to want of affection; for that he looked upon me as his mother! Then he perfumed us all with ottar of roses, and we came away, after thanking him very cordially for his hospitality and the amusement he had given us. I was very curious to see the ladies of the family, but they could not appear before English gentlemen. I peeped about in hopes of catching a glimpse of them, and I did descry some black eyes and white dresses through one of the half-open doors, but I could not see them distinctly.

We are now residing at Rajahmundry, a most lovely spot on the banks of a magnificent river, the Godavery. A. has been appointed judge of this district. I like this place much better than Madras. Every body tried to make Madras as English as they could, though without much success, except doing away with every thing curious; but this place is real India, and I am every day seeing something new and foreign.

We have just returned from a visit to a rajah named Puntooloo. It was a very amusing excursion; and had I known what an undertaking it would be, I never should have attempted it, or rather A. never would have consented to it, however urgent my curiosity might have made me. But we are safe at home again, and the journey has done us good. When the time came for us to go, A. said he thought it would be scarcely worth the trouble, and that we should be "more quiet and comfortable at home"—such a thorough John Bull! But I made him go, as I wished to "see a little of life." The people had told us that the distance was fifteen miles, and we expected that, by starting at half past five in the afternoon, we should arrive about ten o'clock, in time for a good night's rest. But instead of fifteen, we found it to be thirty miles, and no road. We had to grope our way in the dark over cotton fields, the rain pouring down in torrents, and the bearers wading and splashing through the mud, until half past five the next morning, when we arrived at the end of our journey, "plenty tired." We were conducted to a choultry, which the rajah had prepared and ornamented with bits of old carpet for our reception, until he could have us conducted in state to the palace. His principal attendants came to pay their compliments, and he sent us a very good breakfast. When we had eaten, his gomashta (secretary) came to say that all things were ready for our removal. I expected something of a row, but was quite unprepared for the uproar which had been provided for us. As soon as our palankeens were taken into the street, a gang of musicians started up to play before us with all their might — a performance much like one of Rossini's most noisy overtures, played by bagpipes, hurdy gurdies, penny trumpets, and kettle drums, all out of tune. Then came banners, swords, flags, and silver sticks; then heralds, to proclaim our titles, but we could not make out what they were; and then dancing girls. A. looked rather coy at being, as he said, "made such a fool of;" but when the dancing girls began their antics ankle-deep in the mud, the whole turn-out was so excessively absurd that mortal gravity could stand it no longer; and he was obliged to resign himself to his fate, and laugh and be happy, like me.

When we arrived at the palace, the courts were filled with crowds of ragged retainers, and about fifty dancing girls were bobbing and bowing, salaaming and anticking. At last we came to the rajah's own hall, where we found him the pink of Hindu politeness, bestowing more flowers of speech upon us in a quarter of an hour than one could gather in all England in a twelvemonth. He ushered us to the rooms prepared for us, and staid a while to have a talk, surrounded by his retinue. His palace consisted of unpaved courts walled in, and literally ankle-deep in mud. We could not cross them, but all round there was a raised narrow pathway of hard earth, on which we walked, holding on by the wall for fear of slipping into the mud beneath. Our apartments consisted of one of these courts and the rooms belonging to it. At one end was a room, or rather gallery, which they call a hall, open to the court on one side, without any doors or windows, a small room at each end of the large one, and an outer yard for the servants. The other three sides of the square communicated with other courts of the same kind, one opening into the rajah's own hall. In the middle of our gallery there was a wooden alcove overhanging the street, in which Puntooloo sits and smokes when he is alone. The furniture was a table, a carpet, four chairs, two cane sofas, and a footstool. The room was hung with pictures of divinities, by native artists, two French looking glasses, in fine frames, fastened to the wall in their packing cases, the lids being removed for the occasion, and two little shaving glasses, with the quicksilver rubbed off the back. The rajah was very fond of his pictures, and sent for some colored prints of hares and foxes to show us. They had been given him by an Englishman long ago; and the color having been rubbed off in many places, I offered to mend them for him, which greatly pleased him. While I was filling up the holes in his foxes' coats with a little Vandyke brown, he stood by, crossing his hands and exclaiming, "Ah! all same as new! wonderful skill!" and A. took the opportunity to put in his usual lecture concerning the advantages of female education. Puntooloo said he thought it was a very fine thing to teach girls, but that his people were "too much stupid," and did not like it, and he would not go contrary to their prejudices. When we were tired of him, we dismissed him, as the natives think it a great impoliteness to go away until they are desired; therefore, when we had talked as long as we could, A. said that I was going to sleep, for that he (Puntooloo) "must be aware that sleep was a very good thing." That is the proper formula. When the peons come to report their going away to eat their rice, they always inform me that I "must be aware that eating is a very good thing, and necessary to a man's life."

After we were rested and brisk again, the rajah sent us our dinner. We had brought with us, at his request, plates, knives and forks, bread and beer, and he sent us besides all his own messes, native fashion, in brass trays lined with leaves, and a different little conundrum on each leaf, pillaws, quantities of pickles, ten or a dozen varieties of chutnies, different vegetables, and cakes made of cream, pepper, and sugar.

After dinner, Puntooloo took us out to see the town — we in our palankeens and he in his tonjon, his musicians piping and drumming before us. The entire population of the town of course turned out to see the show. The rajah, perceiving that one of

A.'s palankeen doors was shut, stopped the procession, and came to beg that A. would keep both doors open, and show himself to the multitude. The town was built of mud, and the best of the houses were whitewashed. The streets were ankle-deep in mud, washed off from the walls of the houses; but in the midst of all this dirt and discomfort, some little bit of tinsel would show itself at every opportunity — women, covered with ornaments from head to foot, peeping out of the mud hovels; men, with superb Cashmere shawls, looking quite beggarly from rags and dirt. This is "Eastern splendor" — a compound of mud and magnificence, filth and finery. Puntooloo is a great prince in his little way — one of the old hereditary rajahs of the highest caste.

When we returned to the palace, we found it illuminated with torches and crowded with spectators. We staid and witnessed the performances of dancing girls, and the exhibition of fireworks, as long as we could endure the heat, din, and glare, and then went to our own rooms. There we found every thing such a complete contrast to the native taste, that we could scarcely fancy ourselves only a hundred yards from all the rajah's row. Our matee had lighted the candles, and placed our tea things, books, and drawing materials on the table, all looking as quiet and comfortable as at home. I never saw any thing so curiously different from the scene of the minute before; every feeling and idea was changed in an instant.

The next day, Puntooloo introduced me to his wife. I had been longing to see her, but did not dare to ask it for fear of distressing his feelings; however, he proposed it himself. They brought her when A. was out of the room. She was an immense creature, but young, with rather a good, sphinx-like face — altogether, much like a handsome young feather bed. She was dressed in green muslin embroidered with gold, and covered with jewels from top to toe, besides a belt of gold coins round her waist. All her attendant women came with her, and stood at the entrance. The rajah's gomashta stood by, to order her about and teach her manners; and one of my peons acted as interpreter. When she first came in, she twirled, or rather rolled round and round, and did not know what to do until the gomashta bid her make salaam and sit down on a chair, and then I did the same. We did not know much of each other's language — she nothing of mine, and I only enough of hers to be aware that the peon mistranslated every speech we made, and invented the conversation according to his own taste, making it consist entirely of most furious compliments on either side. She was very curious about my clothes, especially my bonnet, which she poised upon her forefinger, and spun round like a top. I showed her some pictures; she held them upside down, and admired them very much. She seemed amused and comfortable till A. came accidentally into the room, when she jumped up, turned her broad back to him, and waddled off as fast as her fat sides would let her. Of course he went away directly, not wishing to hurt her modesty; and as soon as he was gone, she came mincing back again, reseated herself with all sorts of affected airs and graces, and sent him a condescending message to "beg he would not distress himself, for that he was her father and mother."

While she remained with me, A. took the opportunity of being alone with Puntooloo, to try to do him a little good. He was very ready to listen, — unusually so for a Brahmin, — and did not refuse to take some books. I gave him some drawings, which I had made for him, of subjects likely to suit his taste, particularly an eruption of Mount Vesuvius, on account of the red flames. I put the drawings in a blue satin portfolio, embroidered with scarlet and gold; and he was delighted with it.

We came home on a dry night quite safely, and found all well; but an unexpected stranger visitor had arrived while we were absent, and established himself in our house, ready to receive us; however, he was an agreeable person, and we liked his company.

I left off writing just now for my "tiffin," and could not imagine what they were bringing me to eat — some *bran*, which I had been boiling to season a new tin kettle, and which the matee supposed to be some peculiar Europe cooky I was making for myself; and thinking I was provided for, he had eaten up all my meat.